Theodore Roosevelt

Icon of the American Century

James G. Barber

with an essay by Amy Verone
Foreword by John Allen Gable

National Portrait Gallery, Smithsonian Institution
National Park Service, United States Department of the Interior

In association with the University of Washington Press
Seattle and London

This exhibition has been organized by the National Portrait Gallery, Smithsonian Institution, in association with Manhattan Sites and Sagamore Hill National Historic Site, National Park Service, United States Department of the Interior.

Partial support of the exhibition has been provided by grants from the Smithsonian Institution Special Exhibition Fund and the Theodore Roosevelt Association.

EXHIBITION TOUR
NATIONAL PORTRAIT GALLERY, OCTOBER 27, 1998–FEBRUARY 7, 1999
FEDERAL HALL NATIONAL MEMORIAL, NEW YORK CITY, MARCH
    19–JULY 4, 1999
HILLWOOD ART MUSEUM, C. W. POST CAMPUS, LONG ISLAND
    UNIVERSITY, NEW YORK, AUGUST 13–NOVEMBER 14, 1999

©1998 by Smithsonian Institution. All rights reserved.

Library of Congress Cataloging-in-Publication Data
Theodore Roosevelt—Icon of the American Century / James G. Barber; with
    an essay by Amy Verone; foreword by John Allen Gable.
                    p.   cm.
            Exhibition tour: National Portrait Gallery, Oct. 27,
1998–Feb. 7, 1999; Federal Hall National Memorial, New York City,
Mar. 19–July 4, 1999; Hillwood Art Museum, C. W. Post Campus,
Long Island University, N.Y., Aug. 13–Nov. 14, 1999
            "In association with the University of Washington Press,
            Seattle and London."
            Includes bibliographical references.
            ISBN 0-295-97753-1
            1. Roosevelt, Theodore, 1858–1919—Exhibitions. 2.
Roosevelt, Theodore, 1858–1919—Portraits—Exhibitions. 3.
Presidents—United States—Biography—Exhibitions.   I. Barber,
James, 1952– . II. Verone, Amy.   III. National Portrait Gallery
(Smithsonian Institution) IV. United States. National Park Service.
E757.T36   1998
973.91'1'092—dc21
[B]   98-23378
                                        CIP

Cover: Theodore Roosevelt (detail) by John Singer Sargent, 1903. THE WHITE HOUSE, WASHINGTON, D.C. Illustrated in full on page 49.

Half-title page: Theodore Roosevelt (detail) by Edward S. Curtis, 1904. NATIONAL PORTRAIT GALLERY, SMITHSONIAN INSTITUTION, WASHINGTON, D.C. Illustrated in full on page 63.

Frontispiece: Theodore Roosevelt and the Rough Riders at San Juan Heights (detail) by William Dinwiddie, 1898. THEODORE ROOSEVELT COLLECTION, HARVARD COLLEGE LIBRARY, CAMBRIDGE, MASSACHUSETTS; THEODORE ROOSEVELT ESTATE deposit. BY permission OF THE THEODORE ROOSEVELT ASSOCIATION. Illustrated in full on page 38.

Right: In 1884, when Roosevelt "became a cattleman his cowboy outfits dimmed the sunsets of the Western skies," wrote one biographer.*

Theodore Roosevelt by an unidentified photographer, possibly Brown Brothers, New York City, photograph, 20.9 x 15.9 cm. (8¼ x 6¼ in.), circa 1885. THEODORE ROOSEVELT COLLECTION, HARVARD COLLEGE LIBRARY, CAMBRIDGE, MASSACHUSETTS

*Henry F. Pringle, *Theodore Roosevelt: A Biography* (New York, 1931), p. 66.

Contents

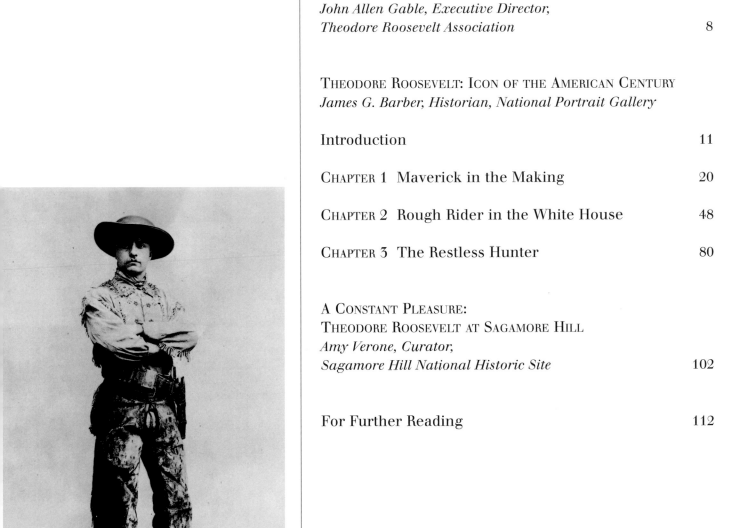

By Roosevelt's last year in the White House, he had long grown tired of requests to sit to photographers and portrait painters. Only as a favor to an old friend from England, Arthur Lee, did he agree to sit for a portrait by the accomplished Hungarian-born artist Philip A. de Lászlo. The sittings took place in the spring of 1908, about which Roosevelt reported enthusiastically to Lee. "I took a great fancy to Lászlo himself," he wrote, "and it is the only picture which I really enjoyed having painted."* Lászlo encouraged the President to invite guests to the sittings to keep Roosevelt entertained. "And if there weren't any visitors," said Roosevelt, "I would get Mrs. Lászlo, who is a trump, to play the violin on the other side of the screen." When the painting was finished, Roosevelt said that he liked it "better than any other."

Ten years later, however, Roosevelt expressed a preference for John Singer Sargent's portrait, done in 1903, which he thought had "a singular quality, a blend of both the spiritual and the heroic."** Still, he thought that Mrs. Roosevelt favored Lászlo's more relaxed image, a trademark of the artist's ingratiating style.

Theodore Roosevelt by Adrian Lamb (1901–1988), after the 1908 oil by Philip Alexius de Lászlo, oil on canvas, 127 x 101.6 cm. (50 x 40 in.), 1967. NATIONAL PORTRAIT GALLERY, SMITHSONIAN INSTITUTION, WASHINGTON, D.C.; GIFT OF THE THEODORE ROOSEVELT ASSOCIATION

*Roosevelt to Arthur Hamilton Lee, April 8, 1908, *The Letters of Theodore Roosevelt*, ed. Elting E. Morison (Cambridge, Mass., 1951–1954), vol. 6, p. 995.
**Roosevelt to Belle Willard Roosevelt, February 2, 1918, ibid., vol. 8, p. 1279.

Lenders to the Exhibition

Harvard College Library, Cambridge, Massachusetts

Library of Congress, Washington, D.C.

Lyndon Baines Johnson Library and Museum, Austin, Texas

Museum of American Art of the Pennsylvania Academy of the Fine Arts, Philadelphia

National Archives, Washington, D.C.

National Museum of American History, Smithsonian Institution, Washington, D.C.

National Museum of Natural History, Smithsonian Institution, Washington, D.C.

National Portrait Gallery, Smithsonian Institution, Washington, D.C.

Private collection

Sagamore Hill National Historic Site, National Park Service, Oyster Bay, New York

Smithsonian Institution Archives, Washington, D.C.

Theodore Roosevelt Association, Oyster Bay, New York

Theodore Roosevelt Birthplace National Historic Site, National Park Service, New York City

Theodore Roosevelt Inaugural Site Foundation, National Park Service, Buffalo, New York

The White House, Washington, D.C.

Foreword

ONE COULD ARGUE that Theodore Roosevelt basically invented, or at least drew up the blueprints for, what came to be called the "American Century." Back when that century was still young, in the years from 1901 to 1909, Theodore Roosevelt, the youngest President in history, brought the federal government into the marketplace and the workplace, fathered conservation and the modern navy, built the Panama Canal, won the Nobel Peace Prize, and preached from the "bully pulpit" of the presidency the doctrines of the "square deal" in domestic policy and "speak softly and carry a big stick" in foreign affairs. The twenty-sixth President created in those years what political scientists call the modern presidency.

Later, as the aging Bull Moose Progressive, TR became the thundering prophet of the welfare state and democratic nationalism through championing such reforms as the presidential primary system, votes for women, and social security insurance to guard against the "hazards of sickness, accident, invalidism, involuntary unemployment, and old age."

In short, it is hard to overestimate TR's importance in seeing and setting the course the country followed in the twentieth century.

So much for Theodore Roosevelt the statesman. To understand TR's full significance, we need also to consider the fact that TR was and is an American hero and icon. He was the frail, asthmatic boy who conquered his own body; the dude from the East who lived the fantasy of being a cowboy in the Wild West; the fearless hunter of grizzly bears and lions; the colonel of the Rough Riders leading the charge in the Battle of San Juan Hill; and the leader who survived a would-be assassin's bullet in the chest and made his scheduled speech. He preached and practiced the "strenuous life." TR was admired and is remembered not only for his achievements as a statesman, but also for being a heroic human being.

Consider this statement by John Hay, TR's secretary of state (and in his youth a secretary to Abraham Lincoln),

"Each man of them knows very well that he could wish no happier lot to his boy in the cradle than that he might grow up to be such a man as Theodore Roosevelt."—JOHN HAY

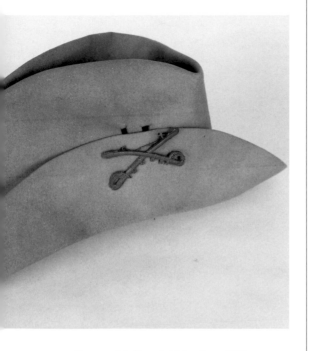

Roosevelt's Rough Rider hat, 1898.
SAGAMORE HILL NATIONAL HISTORIC
SITE, NATIONAL PARK SERVICE, OYSTER
BAY, NEW YORK

speaking about President Roosevelt's political opponents: "Each man of them knows very well that he could wish no happier lot to his boy in the cradle than that he might grow up to be such a man as Theodore Roosevelt."

How many Presidents (or candidates for any office) could play that trump card? Old John Hay could not have made this assertion if there was any possibility of dissent, or any chance of being laughed at. Walter Lippmann once said that he had never been entirely fair to any of TR's successors in the White House because TR was the first President he knew; and perhaps one of the reasons why Americans have made the twentieth century their own is because TR set such high standards at the start of the century.

The National Portrait Gallery has made a good choice in selecting Theodore Roosevelt as the subject for an exhibition as we approach the end of the twentieth century and think about the meaning of this century. TR's image is still with us, on Mount Rushmore, at the five National Park Service sites dedicated to him (Theodore Roosevelt Birthplace in New York City, Sagamore Hill on Long Island, Theodore Roosevelt Island in the Potomac, Theodore Roosevelt National Park in North Dakota, and the Theodore Roosevelt Inaugural National Historic Site in Buffalo, New York), in the books about TR that continue to be published every year, and in the pictures of him that one sees hung on the walls of a surprising number of offices and residences these days.

TR's image is still with us, in part because the old Rough Rider remains a hero to many Americans, and also because, even in this postmodern period, we remain in the historical continuum Theodore Roosevelt helped launch a hundred years ago. To be sure, much about TR seems dated, particularly his stern sense of duty and morality. Yet when we contemplate TR's image, and his meaning and relevance as an icon, we are in a real sense looking at ourselves as Americans.

John Allen Gable
Executive Director
Theodore Roosevelt Association, Oyster Bay, New York

Introduction

After Gutzon Borglum first began designing his monumental carvings of Presidents Washington, Jefferson, and Lincoln for Mount Rushmore, in the Black Hills of South Dakota in 1925, he discovered that there was room for still one more massive head. For Borglum the selection of Theodore Roosevelt was as natural as the mountain of gray granite itself. Borglum had once worked out of a studio in New York City and had made Roosevelt's acquaintance when TR was a police commissioner. The two shared similar interests and philosophies about living robustly. "I do everything—boxing, fencing, wrestling, horseback riding," Borglum once told a journalist. "The trouble with American life is that it is not vigorous enough." The friendship between the two men strengthened during Roosevelt's presidency. In 1911, Roosevelt was the guest speaker at the dedication of Borglum's statue of Lincoln, seated on a bench, near the entrance to City Hall in Newark, New Jersey. The next year, during the presidential contest, Borglum entered the political fray, campaigning for Roosevelt and the Progressive Party. When Borglum suggested Roosevelt's image for Mount Rushmore, critics said that TR was too contemporary. The sculptor argued that Roosevelt had been the defender of the working man, a popular contention which secured his niche on the mountainside forever. This bronze bust of Roosevelt is a version of the original plaster model Borglum used for Mount Rushmore.

Theodore Roosevelt by Gutzon Borglum (1867–1941), bronze, 45.7 cm. (18 in.) height, 1920. SAGAMORE HILL NATIONAL HISTORIC SITE, NATIONAL PARK SERVICE, OYSTER BAY, NEW YORK

"MY CROWDED HOUR" was how Theodore Roosevelt described his adventures as a Rough Rider in Cuba in 1898, while fighting for that island's independence from Spain. Yet this was but one historic episode in what could be called Roosevelt's crowded life. When he died in 1919, at the age of sixty, he was not old, but he was tired. Given his passion for living each day to its fullest, TR had lived the equivalent of several lives, or so it seemed. "I always believe in going hard at everything," he preached time and again; "let us rather run the risk of wearing out than rusting out."[1] This was the basis for living what TR called the "strenuous life," and he exhorted it for the individual and the nation alike.

As the twenty-sixth President of the United States, Theodore Roosevelt was the wielder of the Big Stick, the builder of the Panama Canal, an avid conservationist, and the nemesis of the corporate trusts that threatened to monopolize American business at the start of the century. Yet his presidency accounted for only seven and a half years of a busy life. TR was so much more: political maverick, civic reformer, Rough Rider, governor, cowboy, sportsman, naturalist, historian, man of letters, and defender of the American family. Reading and hunting were his lifelong passions; writing was his lifelong compulsion. When he could combine all three, as he did during his African safari in 1909 and 1910, he was happiest. Only the yearlong separation from his adored wife Edith kept that adventure from being perfect. In dozens of books, monographs, and magazine articles, not to mention thousands of personal letters and state papers, Roosevelt left a prodigious account of himself, his interests, his values, and his views of how human beings should behave toward each other and toward their environment. Naturalist John Burroughs wrote: "Such versatility, such vitality, such thoroughness, such copiousness, have rarely been united in one man."[2]

The life of Theodore Roosevelt (1858–1919) spanned America's transition from a provincial society to a burgeoning world power. Two uncles on his mother's side served the Confederacy during the Civil War. His youngest son, Quentin, was killed in World War I while flying a fighter plane over

France. Roosevelt, a child of the horse-and-buggy age, could not resist taking a ride in an airplane in 1910; and he was the first President to have ridden in an automobile. His philosophy of life in general—about the things that mattered most to him, like family, government, and democracy—was a blend of traditional and progressive thinking. His prescription for the nation—the New Nationalism—was a synthesis of two old, established political points of view. Modern Americans, said Roosevelt, should be "Hamiltonian in their belief in a strong and efficient National Government and Jeffersonian in their belief in the people as the ultimate authority, and in the welfare of the people as the end of the government." In 1912, as the Progressive (or "Bull Moose") Party candidate, TR campaigned for a federal trade commission, unemployment and old-age insurance, and voting rights for women. "Theodore Roosevelt laid the foundations for the way we have been doing things ever since," observed one Roosevelt historian.[5] His life was a bridge between old and new. His patriotism and idealism personified the national spirit at the start of what would be called the "American Century."

Theodore Roosevelt was born on October 27, 1858, in a brownstone house on Twentieth Street in New York City. The original dwelling no longer stands, but a re-creation built on the original site and dedicated in 1923, furnished with Roosevelt family heirlooms, now replicates the domestic tranquillity of TR's earliest years. The child was fortunate in his beginnings and played an active role in his own development. His father, Theodore Roosevelt Sr., was a prosperous merchant, who specialized in importing glassware and was one of the wealthy old Knickerbocker class. His Dutch ancestors had been living on Manhattan Island since the 1640s, when Claes Martenszen van Rosenvelt and his wife stepped ashore on what was then called New Amsterdam. In his *Autobiography*, TR said that his "father was the best man I ever knew."[4] He admired his courage, strength, gentleness, and generosity, all qualities he brought to bear throughout the metropolis. The elder Roosevelt was one of the founders of the New York Orthopedic Hospital, the Children's Aid Society, the Newsboy's Lodging

Theodore Roosevelt Sr. (1831–1878) by Hanfstaengl, Dresden, Germany, cabinet card, 17.1 x 10.8 cm. (6¾ x 4¼ in.), 1873. THEODORE ROOSEVELT COLLECTION, HARVARD COLLEGE LIBRARY, CAMBRIDGE, MASSACHUSETTS

Martha Bulloch Roosevelt (1834–1884) by Robert Eich, Dresden, Germany, cabinet card, 14.6 x 10.8 cm. (5¾ x 4¼ in.), 1873. THEODORE ROOSEVELT COLLECTION, HARVARD COLLEGE LIBRARY, CAMBRIDGE, MASSACHUSETTS

House, the American Museum of Natural History, and the Metropolitan Museum of Art. Although TR never equaled his father as a philanthropist, he did adopt his strong moral code, his sense of civic duty, and his political affiliation with the Republican Party. Theodore Sr. was the "ideal man," a model for TR in every aspect, except for perhaps one. He chose not to join the Union army during the Civil War, and hired a substitute. In part, this was in deference to Mrs. Roosevelt's family ties, and it underscored the familial bond between husband and wife. Theodore's mother, Martha Bulloch, was reputedly one of the loveliest girls to have been born in antebellum Georgia. Her relatives were southern aristocrats, with whom she maintained close personal contact throughout her married life in New York. "Mittie" was meticulous in her person and house; she would routinely take a second bath for rinsing and would cover the furniture with sheets so that strangers would not soil the upholstery. The future Rough Rider never acquired similar habits of fastidiousness, but he did take after his mother in one way: he never learned to manage the family finances.

The parents called their second child Teedie. As an adult, TR claimed that no one who knew him well ever called him Teddy, although the public was wont to do so. An elder sister, Anna, a younger brother, Elliott, and a younger sister, Corinne, comprised the immediate household. Theodore probably took for granted many refinements like the family china and table linen, all adorned with the Roosevelt crest and monogram. Wealth, however, was no substitute for good health, and in this aspect of his childhood the young lad faced life-threatening challenges. He was underweight and often sickly, and his eyesight was poor. Worst of all were the attacks of asthma that left him awake at night and gasping for breath. When holding the boy in his arms brought no relief, the older Roosevelt would take him for carriage rides, thereby forcing fresh air into his lungs. Still, no remedies could stop the attacks. TR had to endure them until his early adulthood.

To strengthen his weak constitution, Theodore lifted dumbbells and exercised in a room of the house converted into a gymnasium. He took boxing lessons to defend himself

Theodore Roosevelt at about the age of
seven, possibly by Rockwood, New York
City, photograph, 20.9 x 15.9 cm. (8¼ x 6¼
in.), circa 1865. THEODORE ROOSEVELT
COLLECTION, HARVARD COLLEGE LIBRARY,
CAMBRIDGE, MASSACHUSETTS

☛

The occasion for this photograph of Alice
Hathaway Lee (1861–1884) and Theodore
Roosevelt, and their friend, Alice's cousin
(and chaperon), Rose Saltonstall (right),
was arranged by Roosevelt himself in May
1879, shortly before he proposed marriage
to Alice. She refused and kept him waiting
anxiously for nearly eight months before
she finally consented. Roosevelt was
finishing his junior year at Harvard when
this image, possibly copied from a tintype,
was made originally.

Alice Hathaway Lee, Theodore
Roosevelt, and Rose Saltonstall by Allen
and Rowell, Boston, cabinet card, 16.5 x
10.8 cm. (6½ x 4¼ in.), 1879. THEODORE
ROOSEVELT COLLECTION, HARVARD COLLEGE
LIBRARY, CAMBRIDGE, MASSACHUSETTS. BY
PERMISSION OF THE HOUGHTON LIBRARY,
HARVARD UNIVERSITY

In this photograph, Roosevelt is in his mid-teens and is wearing a bandanna on his head. His friend and future wife, Edith Kermit Carow, sits in front of him, with Roosevelt's sister, Corinne, and brother, Elliott.

Theodore, Edith, Corinne, and Elliott by an unidentified photographer, tintype, 10.2 x 6.4 cm. (4 x 2½ in.), circa 1875–1876. THEODORE ROOSEVELT COLLECTION, HARVARD COLLEGE LIBRARY, CAMBRIDGE, MASSACHUSETTS

and to test his competitive spirit. By nature, he was never one for turning the other cheek. Roosevelt enjoyed the sport for most of his life; he even boxed as President, until a blow to his head left him blind in one eye.

Natural science, hunting, reading, and writing were all interests that TR had developed in his youth. He shot birds and other wildlife. He stuffed them, sketched them, and recorded his collection in journals, listing each species by its scientific name. The smell of formaldehyde seeping out of his room always alarmed his mother. The family library was a favorite retreat for the youngster, whose curiosity and interests knew no bounds. Roosevelt's childhood diaries reveal much about the quality of his expanding mind. His articulation and penmanship alone are indicative of the care of his home tutoring, which prepared him to enter Harvard University in the fall of 1876.

Roosevelt made the most of his four years in Cambridge. In addition to managing a full schedule of classes, he threw himself into campus clubs and fraternal societies. He edited a college newspaper and was elected to the honor society, Phi Beta Kappa. He exuded energy and enthusiasm in everything, and at times his confidence was overbearing. "See here, Roosevelt, let me talk," cried one instructor. "I'm running this course." His father's death from cancer in 1878 was a shocking blow, and TR was slow to recover his natural verve. When he did, he was in love. "See that girl?" he pointed out to a friend at a party. "I am going to marry her. She won't have me, but I am going to have *her!*"[5] Honey-blond and gray-eyed, Alice Lee had a lively, good mind of her own. She kept TR at arm's length in the beginning. Only by degrees did she warm to his persistent advances and accept invitations to play tennis, to go dancing, and to have a photograph taken of them together. TR proved himself to be a worthy and affectionate suitor. The autumn after he graduated magna cum laude, and on his twenty-second birthday, he and Alice were married in the Unitarian Church in Brookline, Massachusetts.

Amid the intense happiness Roosevelt experienced in his private life during his first year of marriage, he laid the foundations of his historic public career. "I rose like a rocket," he

"See that girl?" he pointed out to a friend at a party. "I am going to marry her. She won't have me, but I am going to have her!"

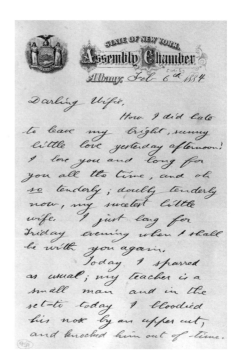

With the birth of his first child imminent, Theodore Roosevelt, in this letter of February 6, 1884, sent from Albany, expressed his desire to be with his wife in New York City. On February 14, two days after giving birth to a daughter, Mrs. Theodore Roosevelt Jr. died of Bright's disease. THEODORE ROOSEVELT COLLECTION, HARVARD COLLEGE LIBRARY, CAMBRIDGE, MASSACHUSETTS. BY PERMISSION OF THE HOUGHTON LIBRARY, HARVARD UNIVERSITY, AND THE THEODORE ROOSEVELT ASSOCIATION

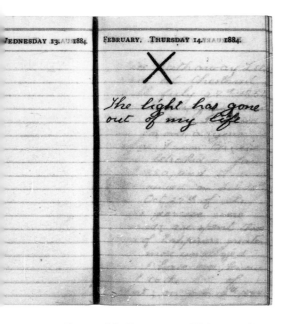

Roosevelt's diary entry of February 14, 1884, the day his wife and mother died in the same house, noted: "The light has gone out of my life." MANUSCRIPT DIVISION, LIBRARY OF CONGRESS, WASHINGTON, D.C.

said years later.[6] Ironically, when he charted his own path for public office—the White House in 1912—he failed bitterly. When others had selected him—as they did for the New York Assembly in 1881, for the governorship in 1898, and for the vice presidency in 1900—his election was almost a foregone conclusion. Politics aside, Roosevelt shaped and molded his life as much as any person could possibly do. He admitted this himself in his vast autobiographical material, both published and private. The plethora of books he wrote, on history and biography, on the West and on hunting, if rarely the last word, were nonetheless the products of incredible will and determination. His first book, *The Naval War of 1812,* was a critical success. He began writing it in college and finished it eighteen months after graduation. Meanwhile, he was attending law school at Columbia University, and he had embarked on a delayed European honeymoon in the summer of 1881. When he delivered the manuscript to the publisher that December, he was preparing to take his seat in the state assembly at the capitol in Albany. His new and sudden calling came as a jolt to his genteel family, not used to the "rough and tumble" of entry-level politics.[7] For the Roosevelts, and especially for TR in these early years, the only thing more unpredictable than politics was life itself, and it turned agonizingly cruel on Valentine's Day 1884. In less than twenty-four hours, and in the same house at 6 West Fifty-seventh Street, Roosevelt's mother died of typhoid fever and his wife died of Bright's disease, two days after giving birth to a daughter, Alice Lee. "For joy or sorrow," Roosevelt wrote in his diary, "my life has now been lived out."[8] As she grew more handsome and precocious with each passing year, young Alice would cause her father both joy and anxiety. But contrary to his diary, TR's life was still in its formative stages, as his career was just getting started. On the heels of personal tragedy, TR was on the verge of becoming a national presence.

Theodore Roosevelt was the most captivating American in public life between the Civil War and New Deal eras. Abraham Lincoln and Franklin D. Roosevelt were products of their troubled times; TR was largely the product of his irrepressible self:

"Do you know the two most wonderful things I have seen in your country?" observed the English statesman John Morley: "Niagara Falls and the President of the United States, both great wonders of nature!" Roosevelt's presence was irresistible. When he was "in the neighborhood," one reporter noted, the public could "no more look the other way than the small boy can turn his head away from a circus parade followed by a steam calliope." The closer one got to him, the greater was his attraction. "You go to the White House, you shake hands with Roosevelt and hear him talk—and then go home to wring the personality out of your clothes," said one guest. With TR, the luster of the presidency never outshone his own magnetism. He carried it into the executive mansion and out of it. In 1917, Richard Henry Dana III was sitting next to Roosevelt at the Harvard Club of New York, and "for half an hour I basked in the sunlight glow he shed about him."[9]

The light always came from within, because TR was an ordinary-looking man. He became stout as an adult, a fact clearly in evidence in hundreds of photographs, and was in the prime of his life as President. Individuals standing in height a few inches under six feet could look dead level into his pale blue eyes, if the sun was not glinting off his spectacles. His mouth was noteworthy only for its constant animation; he gave the impression of being able to talk and to listen simultaneously. His teeth were prominent, because he showed them a lot, characteristically with good nature. "By George," Roosevelt once exclaimed, "I don't believe I ever do talk with a man five minutes without liking him very much, unless I disliked him very much." His brown and gray-speckled hair was stiff and often cropped unflatteringly close, especially in later years. A sizeable girth about his chest made him look heavier than two hundred pounds. Roosevelt wore a mustache all his adult life, which grayed and bristled with age and gave him a walrus-like appearance when he habitually grinned and squinted. Near the end of Roosevelt's life, a young admirer tried to fathom his charm. "I wonder," she wrote, "how a man so thick-set, of rather abdominal contour, with eyes heavily spectacled, could have had so much an air of magic and wild romance about him, could give one so stirring an impression of adventure and chivalry."[10]

"By George," Roosevelt once exclaimed, "I don't believe I ever do talk with a man five minutes without liking him very much, unless I disliked him very much."

1. Edmund Morris, *The Rise of Theodore Roosevelt* (New York, 1979), p. 661; *Theodore Roosevelt Cyclopedia*, ed. Albert Bushnell Hart and Herbert Ronald Ferleger (Westport, Conn., 1989), p. 587.

2. *TR Cyclopedia*, p. v.

3. Ibid., p. xviii.

4. Theodore Roosevelt, *An Autobiography* (New York, 1913), pp. 1–9.

5. Henry F. Pringle, *Theodore Roosevelt: A Biography* (New York, 1931), pp. 33, 42.

6. Ibid., p. 73.

7. Morris, *Roosevelt*, p. 143.

8. Ibid., p. 244.

9. Ibid., pp. 20, 26–27; Edward Wagenknecht, *The Seven Worlds of Theodore Roosevelt* (New York, 1958), pp. 108–9.

10. Wagenknecht, *Seven Worlds*, pp. 105, 110.

11. Ibid., p. 107; Nathan Miller, *Theodore Roosevelt: A Life* (New York, 1992), p. 411.

12. Maurice Horn, ed., *The World Encyclopedia of Cartoons* (New York, 1980), vol. 2, p. 784.

13. Mark Sullivan, *Our Times, 1900–1925*, vol. 3 (New York, 1930), p. 75.

14. *TR Cyclopedia*, p. xiii.

Caption:
Page 11: "I do everything," in Donald Dale Jackson, "Gutzon Borglum's Odd and Awesome Portraits in Granite," *Smithsonian* 23 (August 1992): 68.

Theodore Roosevelt had the "quality of vitalizing things," and this is what captivated individuals and the country alike. From the start of his public career as a political reformer, he made news and later headlines. He had a way of "slapping the public on the back with a bright idea," said one editor.[11] Roosevelt put a cut-and-dried issue like civil service reform on the front pages. The presidency itself has never vacated the spotlight since he left office in 1909.

By chance, Roosevelt gained national prominence just as America's humorous weeklies, notably *Puck, Judge,* and *Life,* were vying for readers of political and social satire. These were popular magazines with a wide appeal and a profound influence. One authority has written, "Many reforms—civil service, tariff, currency, railroads, armaments—were explained to a mass audience in sophisticated cartoons that were worth thousands of tracts and speeches."[12] In the hands of the country's best comic artists—Joseph Keppler, Eugene Zimmerman, and Will Crawford, to name but three—TR personified all of these issues and more. Between 1898 and 1919, no American was better known or more ubiquitous. When TR was President, he routinely received mail addressed only with drawings of teeth and spectacles. In 1910, three cartoon histories of Roosevelt's career were published. This was prior to the historic "Bull Moose" campaign, which inspired dozens more of some of TR's most memorable cartoons. One source compared this grand outpouring to a phenomenon of nature: "At any gusty word from him, cartoons filled the air like autumn leaves in a high wind."[13]

Now, a century after Theodore Roosevelt was living the strenuous life, Americans continue to live his legacy. Such reforms as meat inspection, railroad regulation, and the conservation of national forests and wetlands—which are now mostly taken for granted—were all Roosevelt's initiatives. TR even founded the National Collegiate Athletic Association. And what American child has never had a teddy bear? The images that comprise this exhibition and catalogue offer a glimpse of the man who, in his day, was deemed "the most interesting American."[14]

Chapter 1

Maverick in the Making

T HEODORE ROOSEVELT made a difference from the start of his political career. Between 1882 and 1884, he represented the Twenty-first District of New York City in the state legislative assembly in Albany. An 1881 campaign broadside noted that the young Republican candidate was "conspicuous for his honesty and integrity," qualities not taken for granted in a city run by self-serving machine politicians. In appearance alone, he stood out when he took his seat in the assembly chamber. One colleague recalled, "His hair was parted in the center, and he had sideburns. He wore a single eye-glass, with a gold chain over his ear. He had on a cutaway coat with one button at the top, and the ends of its tails almost reached the tops of his shoes. He carried a gold-headed cane in one hand, a silk hat in the other, and he walked in the bent over fashion that was the style with young men of the day. His trousers were as tight as a tailor could make them, and had a bell-shaped bottom to cover his shoes.

'Who's the dude?' one assemblyman asked another.
'That's Theodore Roosevelt of New York.'"[1]

On the occasion of TR's maiden speech, the press noted that he spoke with a quaint "Dundreary drawl"; about the issue at hand, Roosevelt said that his constituents were feeling "r-a-w-t-h-e-r r-e-l-i-e-v-e-d." His social standing and Harvard education contrasted sharply with the eight Tammany Hall Democrats who represented the machine in control of

TR's reform politics often drew the ire of machine politicians, as illustrated in this image.

The Glad Hand by R. L. Bristol (lifedates unknown), watercolor and ink on paper, 40.7 x 35.6 cm. (16 x 14 in.), for *Verdict*, April 16, 1900. THEODORE ROOSEVELT BIRTHPLACE NATIONAL HISTORIC SITE, NATIONAL PARK SERVICE, NEW YORK CITY

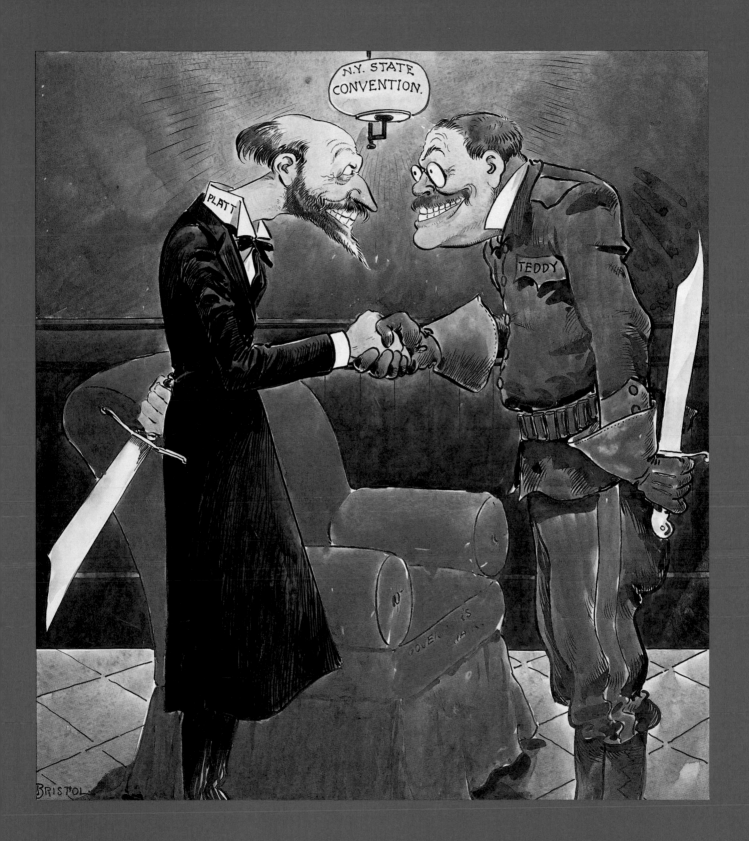

much of New York City. Roosevelt described them as being "totally unable to speak with even an approximation to good grammar; not even one of them can string three intelligible sentences together to save his neck." He suspected that one of these men, "a huge, fleshy, unutterably coarse and low brute," had "begun his life as a pickpocket."[2] Overall, he guessed that about one-third of his cohorts in the assembly were corrupt.

In his *Autobiography,* Roosevelt believed that his third and last session in the legislature, that of 1884, was his most significant. The popular illustrated newspapers corroborated this view. That winter and spring, Roosevelt began appearing, sometimes on the covers, in the leading political journals of the country. On February 20, four days after he buried his wife and mother in historic Greenwood Cemetery, he was caricatured on the cover of *Puck,* shearing the claws off of the Tammany tiger, emblem of the Democratic machine. This was in reference to a municipal reform bill—one of several he introduced that winter—that would increase the power of New York City's mayor. As things then stood, the city's twenty-four aldermen, backed by one machine or another, had confirming power over the mayor's appointments. Roosevelt argued that if the mayor were made more independent, the electorate, not the machines, would stand to gain. His bill won wide public support, as well as significant opposition in the assembly. Roosevelt initiated and then became the chairman of a special committee to investigate corruption in the city government. In a wood engraving in the April 17 issue of *Life,* titled *Bravo!,* Roosevelt swings an axe at a "deadly upas" tree labeled "city government." Its branches represent such offices as the treasurer, sheriff, police, mayor, public works, and the aldermen.

After Roosevelt successfully maneuvered his reform bills through the assembly, the only thing to prevent sweeping changes in how the city would be run in the future was a veto from the Democratic governor, Grover Cleveland. Indefatigable and honest, Cleveland was a friend of reform; he had already worked successfully with TR for civil service reform. A full-page cartoon in the April 19 *Harper's Weekly* predicted more cooperation. The dean of illustrated political commentary, Thomas Nast, portrayed TR holding his "Reform

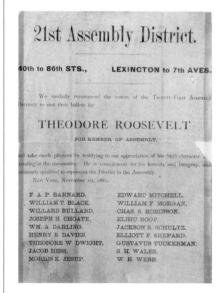

The political memorabilia, campaign buttons, broadsides, banners, and bandannas associated with Theodore Roosevelt's long career of elected public service is extensive. This 1881 broadside, endorsing Roosevelt for a state assembly seat, is the earliest extant document of its kind. THEODORE ROOSEVELT BIRTHPLACE NATIONAL HISTORIC SITE, NATIONAL PARK SERVICE, NEW YORK CITY

Bravo! by an unidentified artist, wood engraving, 52.1 x 31.1 cm. (20½ x 12¼ in.), for *Life*, April 17, 1884. THEODORE ROOSEVELT BIRTHPLACE NATIONAL HISTORIC SITE, NATIONAL PARK SERVICE, NEW YORK CITY

☛

In this photograph of Roosevelt as a second-term assemblyman, gone forever are the muttonchop sideburns that had characterized his appearance since his college days. As a young man, Roosevelt preferred to be photographed without his spectacles.

Theodore Roosevelt by Notman Photographic Company, Albany, New York (active 1878–1927), albumen silver print, 14.1 x 10.3 cm. (5⁹/₁₆ x 4¹/₁₆ in.), 1883. NATIONAL PORTRAIT GALLERY, SMITHSONIAN INSTITUTION, WASHINGTON, D.C.; GIFT OF JOANNA STURM

☛

Reform Without Bloodshed by Thomas Nast (1840–1902), wood engraving, 36.8 x 23.8 cm. (14½ x 9⅜ in.), for *Harper's Weekly,* April 19, 1884. THEODORE ROOSEVELT COLLECTION, HARVARD COLLEGE LIBRARY, CAMBRIDGE, MASSACHUSETTS

Bills" for the governor to sign. Cleveland, however, was an experienced lawyer and read everything carefully before dipping his pen. What he discovered were inconsistencies in Roosevelt's hastily scribbled bills. He could not sign them as written, and Roosevelt was reduced to revising. In the end, seven of his nine reform bills introduced that year were enacted into law.

Roosevelt declined renomination to a fourth term. Exhausted and still adjusting to the death of his wife, he desperately sought a change in his life. That he could not escape politics immediately was a measure of how fast he had risen. Politically, New York was the most important state in the Union; it had given rise to the careers of many national leaders, including President Chester Arthur and the new Democratic challenger, Grover Cleveland. As the state's most promising young politician, Roosevelt was elected a delegate-at-large to the Republican National Convention in Chicago in June 1884. Together with a new ally from Massachusetts, Henry Cabot Lodge, Roosevelt and a party of independents led a futile fight to stop the nomination of James G. Blaine of Maine, a nonreformer whose past as Speaker of the U.S. House of Representatives was tainted with scandal arising from his alleged complicity in illegal railroad stocks. But rather than bolt to the Democratic Party, as did a faction of the independents called the Mugwumps, Roosevelt supported Blaine unenthusiastically in the fall campaign, jeopardizing what he thought would be any future career in public office.

Politics aside, diversion and adventure were Roosevelt's primary motives for traveling to the West in 1884. This would be the first of three occasions during his life when he would seek solace in a remote frontier. After breaking up his family home and leaving baby Alice to the care of his sister, Roosevelt ventured into a desolate, windswept region of the Dakota Territory called the Bad Lands. "Black care rarely sits behind a rider whose pace is fast enough," TR wrote in *Ranch Life and the Hunting Trail*, one of three books in which he related his western experiences. If only for a year or two, TR intended to shake the melancholy from his life. He became the owner of

Roosevelt's political alliance with Henry Cabot Lodge (1850–1924) of Massachusetts began in 1884, when the two were delegates to the Republican National Convention in Chicago. In time, both men would become leaders of the Republican Party. Their extensive mutual correspondence is an insightful record of shared interests and American idealism at the turn of the twentieth century. After serving in the United States House of Representatives for six years, Lodge became a senator in 1893 and retained his seat for the rest of his life. Like Roosevelt, Lodge was an advocate of civil service reform (he recommended Roosevelt to be a commissioner in 1889), a strong navy, the Panama Canal, and pure food and drug legislation. A specialist in foreign affairs, Lodge acted as one of Roosevelt's principal advisers during his presidency. Yet Lodge did not support many of Roosevelt's progressive reforms—women's suffrage, for instance—and he refused to endorse his friend in the Bull Moose campaign of 1912.

Henry Cabot Lodge by John Singer Sargent (1856–1925), oil on canvas, 127 x 86.4 cm. (50 x 34 in.), 1890. NATIONAL PORTRAIT GALLERY, SMITHSONIAN INSTITUTION, WASHINGTON, D.C.; GIFT OF THE HONORABLE HENRY CABOT LODGE

two ranches near the Little Missouri River and the town of Medora. He grazed cattle, proving himself as rugged as the native ranchers. He endured the snow and ice of subzero winters, and he won the respect, sometimes with his bare knuckles, of snickering cowboys who called him Four Eyes. "When I went among strangers I always had to spend twenty-four hours in living down the fact that I wore spectacles," TR wrote in his *Autobiography*.[3] He read Leo Tolstoy's *Anna Karenina* while successfully tracking down three ranch thieves, and he wrote a biography of Senator Thomas Hart Benton of Missouri. And he hunted, almost daily in good weather, to keep food on his table.

Try as he might to become a westerner, TR could never shed his eastern persona. His manner of speaking often betrayed him. On one occasion he told a fellow cowhand, "Hasten forward quickly there!" The man's comrades reeled with laughter, which in turn echoed in barrooms throughout the territory. Even Roosevelt's dress had an air of haughtiness. "You would be amused to see me," he wrote to his friend Henry Cabot Lodge, "in my broad sombrero hat, fringed and beaded buckskin shirt, horse hide chaparajos or riding trousers, and cowhide boots, with braided bridle and silver spurs." Photographs show him fitted out "in the most expensive style," wearing a pearl-hilted revolver and holster.[4] The image of the Tiffany cowboy was made complete with a repoussé silver and engraved steel hunting knife, designed and crafted by the venerable New York jeweler.

On a visit back to New York in the fall of 1885, Roosevelt by chance renewed his friendship with Edith Kermit Carow, a childhood companion. If not the arresting beauty that Alice was, Edith was alluring in a deeper way. She had a pleasing face one never tired of contemplating; a slender, straight nose and a pearly complexion gave her the profile of a Greek goddess. Photographs reveal that she had an hourglass figure enhanced by the fashionable corsets of the day. Intelligent and strong willed, she was a worthy foil for an erudite cowboy such as Roosevelt, and he was captivated. Here was the tomboy of his youth, all finished and polished and still unat-

The buckskin suit Roosevelt is wearing in this photograph was made especially for him by a seamstress living in the Bad Lands, whose specialty was making frontier clothing. Roosevelt made a round-trip of fifty miles on horseback in a single day to collect his new suit. During a visit back to New York at Christmas in 1884, he posed for several studio photographs, including the image here, which appeared as an engraved frontispiece for his first book on the West, *Hunting Trips of a Ranchman*, in 1885. Of this image, Roosevelt wrote in 1901, "It is I think the best photograph of myself in hunting costume that there is."

Theodore Roosevelt by an unidentified photographer, possibly George Grantham Bain, photograph, 21 x 15.9 cm. (8¼ x 6¼ in.), 1885. THEODORE ROOSEVELT COLLECTION, HARVARD COLLEGE LIBRARY, CAMBRIDGE, MASSACHUSETTS

Veteran cartoonist Thomas Nast was nearing the end of his brilliant career with *Harper's Weekly* when he began portraying Theodore Roosevelt. Like Roosevelt, Nast was a reformer. He reached the zenith of his influence in 1871, through a series of cartoons lampooning William Marcy ("Boss") Tweed and his corrupt New York political machine, Tammany Hall. But a decade hence, Nast's black-and-white wood engravings began to lose their appeal compared to the full-color cartoons appearing in magazines like *Puck* and *Judge*. Nast's more lifelike depictions, as they applied to Roosevelt, looked flat compared to the imaginative caricature that was just beginning to appear in rival publications.

Thomas Nast, self-portrait, pencil and india ink on paper, 36.1 x 27 cm. (14 1/16 x 10 5/8 in.), circa 1882. NATIONAL PORTRAIT GALLERY, SMITHSONIAN INSTITUTION, WASHINGTON, D.C.

tached. So began the stampede of Roosevelt's heart back east. He proposed after a courtship of only a few months, and she accepted. The wedding took place the following year in London, far removed from anything possibly associated with Alice. Cecil Spring-Rice, an aspiring young British diplomat whom TR had befriended on the voyage to England, was asked to be best man. "Springy" became a friend for life.

Another European honeymoon revitalized TR's spirits before he returned to his ranches in the Bad Lands to appraise the devastation to his cattle wrought by the unusually severe winter of 1887. For miles he walked without seeing a live animal. Fortunately, his life was centered in the East again, where he settled down to domesticity in a new, multigabled house, Sagamore Hill, overlooking Oyster Bay, Long Island. Two more books flowed from his pen, *The Life of Gouverneur Morris* and *Essays on Practical Politics,* both published in 1888. For his support that year of the successful Republican presidential candidate, Benjamin Harrison, he was rewarded with an appointment to the United States Civil Service Commission. What Harrison viewed as just a perfunctory government office, immersed in the cumbersome Washington bureaucracy, Roosevelt made aggressively active and viable. He evaluated application procedures for fairness and improved testing requirements by making them more practical. At every opportunity—and there were plenty—he challenged the entrenched spoils system of rewarding political stalwarts with federal jobs. He personally inspected post offices in New York City and throughout the Midwest. In 1892, as a result of Roosevelt's urging, a congressional committee investigated the Baltimore postmaster's office, where significant numbers of protected civil servants had been dismissed. The investigation's findings hurt President Harrison's chances for reelection, but he did not risk removing his popular commissioner.

From the start, Roosevelt dominated his two senior commissioners. "I have made this Commission a living force," he wrote to Henry Cabot Lodge in late June 1889, "and in consequence the outcry among the spoilsmen has become furious;

it has evidently frightened . . . the President . . . a little." Roosevelt was determined to do his duty. "I am perfectly willing to be turned out," he added, "but while in I mean business."[5]

Louis Dalrymple, an illustrator for *Puck*, had seemingly been looking over Roosevelt's shoulder when he wrote that letter. His cover illustration for July 10, 1889, depicted TR as the "Brave Little Giant-Killer," challenging the "Spoils-System Giant" with a sword labeled "Civil Service Rules." President Harrison, grasping the sheath of Roosevelt's sword, takes

cover behind a rock, while the Giant warns: "Calm yourself, Theodore. If you go too far, you'll find yourself jerked back mighty sudden by President Harrison!" This warning reflected Roosevelt's own view. The administration, he wrote, has "shown symptoms of telling me that the law should be rigidly enforced where people will stand it, and gingerly handled elsewhere."

To brand cattle belonging to his Elkhorn Ranch, Roosevelt used two different designs, a triangle and an elkhorn, shown here. SAGAMORE HILL NATIONAL HISTORIC SITE, NATIONAL PARK SERVICE, OYSTER BAY, NEW YORK

Roosevelt built his Elkhorn Ranch house on a low bluff overlooking the broad and shallow Missouri River, in the Dakota Territory. The house was made of hewn logs and had a veranda, where Roosevelt enjoyed reading in a rocking chair and shooting at game. This photograph, probably taken by Roosevelt himself, offers a glimpse of his lifestyle. Amid the elkhorns and rocking chairs are his saddle, his pistol and holster, and his rifle. "I do not believe there ever was any life more attractive to a vigorous young fellow than life on a cattle ranch," he wrote in his *Autobiography*. "I enjoyed the life to the full."

Elkhorn Ranch house attributed to Theodore Roosevelt, cabinet card, 10.8 x 15.9 cm. (4¼ x 6¼ in.), 1886. THEODORE ROOSEVELT COLLECTION, HARVARD COLLEGE LIBRARY, CAMBRIDGE, MASSACHUSETTS

Love of adventure and the great outdoors, especially in the West, were the bonds that sealed the friendship between Theodore Roosevelt and Frederic Remington. "I wish I were with you out among the sage brush, the great brittle cottonwoods, and the sharply-channeled barren buttes," Roosevelt wrote to the western artist in 1897 from Washington. In 1888, *Century Magazine* published a series of articles about the West written by Roosevelt and illustrated by Remington. In a May article, Roosevelt told the story of his daring capture of three thieves who had stolen a boat from his Elkhorn Ranch. Remington depicted their capture in this painting.

Hands Up!—The Capture of Finnigan by Frederic Remington (1861–1909), oil on panel, 36 x 42.9 cm. (14⁵/₁₆ x 16⅞ in.), circa 1888. THE WHITE HOUSE, WASHINGTON, D.C.

Roosevelt's hunting knife had a sterling silver repoussé sheath and handle, ornamented with his full name. The engraved steel blade reveals hard use.

Hunting knife and sheath designed and made by Tiffany & Co., knife, 35 cm. (13¾ in.), sheath, 22 cm. (8⅝ in.), 1884. PRIVATE COLLECTION

This cartoon underscores Roosevelt's unflinching courage as a civil service commissioner in ending the spoils system, which rewarded political stalwarts with federal jobs, too often at the expense of long-term workers.

The Brave Little Giant-Killer by Louis Dalrymple (1861–1905), chromolithograph, 25.4 x 24.1 cm. (10 x 9½ in.), for *Puck*, July 10, 1889. THEODORE ROOSEVELT COLLECTION, HARVARD COLLEGE LIBRARY, CAMBRIDGE, MASSACHUSETTS

In spite of President Harrison's faltering commitment, Roosevelt enforced the laws he had pledged to uphold, and he gave civil service reform the impetus it needed to grow and become accepted by the public and the politicians alike. Roosevelt received greater support beginning in 1893 from the new President, Grover Cleveland. Yet by the spring of 1895, TR was once again feeling restless. He had enjoyed his six years in Washington immensely, taking advantage of the capital's full social calendar, in addition to the collections of the Smithsonian Institution. Among his friends and acquaintances he now counted statesman John Hay, historian Henry Adams, and Speaker of the House Thomas Reed. His civil service experience had given him a national perspective, as well as an insight into the dynamics of how the government really functioned. Except for the presidency, he would not hold any other job for as long.

In May 1895, the opportunity to serve on the board of police commissioners of New York City was a welcome challenge for Roosevelt, who was happy to be associated again with his old constituents. Yet much of the appeal stemmed from the reform promises of the new mayor, William L. Strong. Roosevelt was elected president of the four-member board and presided over the reorganization of the police

This photograph of Edith Kermit Carow (1861–1948) was taken about the time she became engaged to Theodore Roosevelt.

Edith Carow by J. Ludovici, New York City, photograph, 15.9 x 10.8 cm. (6¼ x 4¼ in.), 1885. THEODORE ROOSEVELT COLLECTION, HARVARD COLLEGE LIBRARY, CAMBRIDGE, MASSACHUSETTS

The administration, he wrote, has "shown symptoms of telling me that the law should be rigidly enforced where people will stand it, and gingerly handled elsewhere."

department, ridding it of much graft and bribery. Under him, members of the force could no longer buy their promotions; merit and duty were now what counted most. Consequently, department morale and efficiency improved. Patrolmen on night duty now faced an unexpected threat, as Roosevelt, disguised in a dark cloak and broad-brimmed hat, roamed the city beats looking for slackers. The local press delighted in reporting his escapades of catching patrols drinking on the job or mingling with prostitutes. Cartoons showed him surprising napping policemen and warding off with a nightstick party bosses, who were bringing the city to its knees. TR was receiving favorable press elsewhere as well. The *Chicago Times-Herald* reported that he was the biggest man in New York, "if not the most interesting man in public life." And in Ithaca, New York, the local paper named him to be the Republican presidential nominee in 1896.[6]

Roosevelt would have to wait his turn, but the election of William McKinley to the White House that year had political consequences for TR as well. After only two years as a police commissioner, Roosevelt had all but exhausted his reform measures, as well as the patience of many former supporters. His enforcement of the city's unpopular liquor laws, particularly the ban on Sunday saloon sales, irked the drinking public and many elected officials. His overbearing sense of civic duty had split the police board, making it contentious and less effective. When McKinley offered Roosevelt the post of assistant secretary of the navy in the spring of 1897, he readily left for Washington. "Roosevelt came down here looking for war," recalled one member of the House Naval Affairs Committee. "He did not care whom we fought as long as there was a scrap." With the start of the Spanish-American War the following April, Roosevelt was determined to link his family's name with military valor.[7]

Yet he had good reasons to stay out of the fighting. His administrative abilities were a genuine asset in the Navy Department, in spite of his penchant for overstepping bounds. The most memorable instance occurred on February 15, 1898, following the sinking of the battleship *Maine*. Roosevelt, in the

Jacob Riis (1849–1914) was a valuable friend and source of information for Roosevelt when he became a police commissioner in the spring of 1895. As a police reporter for the *New York Evening Sun,* Riis understood the reforms needed within the police department, as well as the evils in the slums, which he frequented to gather stories. Riis was successful in awakening public awareness to the plight of New York's tenement population, especially the children, in several books, including his classic *How the Other Half Lives.* In 1904 Riis published a biography of his good friend, with whom he used to walk the streets of New York, titled *Theodore Roosevelt: The Citizen.*

Jacob Riis by an unidentified photographer, gelatin silver print, 24.5 x 14.2 cm. (9 $^{11}/_{16}$ x 5⅝ in.), circa 1900. NATIONAL PORTRAIT GALLERY, SMITHSONIAN INSTITUTION, WASHINGTON, D.C.; GIFT OF HOWARD GREENBERG

The Sequel—The Dutch Patrol Catches 'Em Napping by Leon Barritt (lifedates unknown), pen and ink, 40.6 x 55.3 cm. (16 x 21¾ in.), for the *New York Advertiser,* June 8, 1895. THEODORE ROOSEVELT BIRTHPLACE NATIONAL HISTORIC SITE, NATIONAL PARK SERVICE, NEW YORK CITY

Roosevelt carried this nightstick when he was a police commissioner in New York in 1895. THEODORE ROOSEVELT BIRTHPLACE NATIONAL HISTORIC SITE, NATIONAL PARK SERVICE, NEW YORK CITY

absence of his superior and in violation of department procedures, ordered Commodore George Dewey to ready his Pacific fleet and to take the offensive against the Spanish squadron in the Philippine Islands, in the event of an American declaration of war. Although premature, Roosevelt's order anticipated the President's own by two months.

Family concerns should also have been a strong inducement for him to have stayed at home. He was now the father of six children. His wife Edith was just recovering from a serious illness after the birth of their child, Quentin. He was six months old when TR resigned his office in the Navy Department to organize a volunteer cavalry regiment, which the press called Roosevelt's Rough Riders. Friends and family, even the newspapers, questioned his judgment. "He has lost his head," wrote his superior, Secretary of the Navy John D. Long. Yet given Roosevelt's sense of duty, there was no keeping him out of the fight: "I have preached it for some time, and I wanted to practice what I preached." He ordered an "ordinary cavalry lieutenant colonel's uniform in blue Cravenette"

Assistant Secretary of the Navy Theodore
Roosevelt by an unidentified
photographer, photograph, 22.9 x 19.7 cm.
(9 x 7¾ in.), circa 1898. THEODORE
ROOSEVELT COLLECTION, HARVARD COLLEGE
LIBRARY, CAMBRIDGE, MASSACHUSETTS

Overleaf
Page 36:
Before leaving the Navy Department in early May 1898, in preparation for organizing his regiment of Rough Riders, Roosevelt wrote a congratulatory letter to Commodore George Dewey (1837–1917) for his masterful victory over Spain's Asiatic Squadron at Manila Bay, Philippines. Dewey destroyed the enemy's entire fleet without the loss of one American sailor. Promoted to admiral after the battle, Dewey became a war hero, much like Roosevelt was destined to become. Yet Dewey lacked the Rough Rider's engaging personality to capitalize politically on his fame. Although he expressed a willingness to be a candidate for President in 1900, neither party considered him.

Rear Admiral George Dewey, U.S.N. The Hero of the Manila Fight by an unidentified artist, after a photograph, lithograph on silk, 52.4 x 52.7 cm. (20⅝ x 20¾ in.), 1898. NATIONAL PORTRAIT GALLERY, SMITHSONIAN INSTITUTION, WASHINGTON, D.C.

Page 37:
Theodore Roosevelt and Leonard Wood (1860–1927) liked each other from their first meeting, in the spring of 1897. Both were robust and athletic, and both, from the vantage points of their respective jobs—Roosevelt as assistant secretary of the navy, and Wood as an army officer (and the physician of President and Mrs. William McKinley)—took a belligerent attitude toward Spain with respect to Cuba. When Roosevelt was offered the chance to raise a regiment of volunteer cavalry, he in turn recruited the more experienced Wood to be the regiment's colonel and commander. After the war in Cuba, Wood remained as military governor of Santiago, and shortly thereafter was appointed to administer the affairs of the entire island.

Leonard Wood by John Singer Sargent (1856–1925), oil on canvas, 76.5 x 63.8 cm. (30⅛ x 25⅛ in.), 1903. NATIONAL PORTRAIT GALLERY, SMITHSONIAN INSTITUTION, WASHINGTON, D.C.

from Brooks Brothers in New York and made arrangements for the purchase of "a couple of good, stout, quiet horses," which "must not be gun-shy." He lingered in Washington that April and early May long enough to wrap up business in the Navy Department and to facilitate the organizing of his regiment, which would be mustered presently in San Antonio. His letters at this time reveal a youthful zeal to join them in Texas.[8] His overriding concern, however, was to get into the fight in Cuba before the war was over.

Events that spring and summer would ultimately work in his favor. The siege of the port city of Santiago, which lasted little more than two weeks, was ideal for Roosevelt, the adventurer and Rough Rider. It was just short enough for him to glory in battle before disease and death ruined the experience, and long enough for him to win a coveted place in American military annals. Leading a motley regiment of former cowboys, Indians, college athletes, and a few New York City policemen, Roosevelt drove the Spanish off of Kettle Hill, a strategic stronghold in the San Juan highlands overlooking Santiago. The fighting was often fierce; Roosevelt claimed that the Rough Riders lost about seven times more men than the other five regiments. He recounted the exploits of his unit, the First Volunteer Cavalry Regiment, in *The Rough Riders,* published in 1899. One reviewer jested that he should have titled the book "Alone in Cuba." Yet Roosevelt gave full credit to his superiors, especially to the regiment's first commander, Colonel Leonard Wood, a veteran Indian fighter and recipient of the Congressional Medal of Honor. (Upon Wood's promotion to brigadier general, TR became the commander of the regiment at the rank of colonel.) Still, only military historians will recall their roles in detail. Indicative of what most people remember of the war in Cuba is the photograph of TR with his victorious Rough Riders atop San Juan Hill. "San Juan was the great day of my life," he recalled twenty years later.[9]

For the Americans, the war with Spain was a popular foreign policy initiative. The country acquired the Philippine Islands, Guam, and Puerto Rico. Admiral Dewey became the hero of Manila Bay, and Theodore Roosevelt, the hero of San

Rear Admiral George Dewey, U. S. N.

THE HERO OF THE MANILA FIGHT.

Juan Hill, was well on his way to becoming legendary. His name was being mentioned for the governorship of New York, and even for the presidency. Full-page photoengravings of him, dressed in his khaki uniform, campaign hat, and navy blue and white polka-dot neckerchief appeared on the covers and inside such popular weekly journals as *Harper's* and *Leslie's.* Roosevelt would wear the image of a Rough Rider for the rest of his life. "I would honestly rather have my position of colonel," he told his men before they were mustered out, "than any other position on earth."[10] Although he would enjoy being President even more, he still wanted to be called "Colonel" after leaving the White House.

That Roosevelt's nomination for governor of New York

Roosevelt posed for this photograph at Montauk, Long Island, shortly before his First Volunteer Cavalry Regiment was mustered out of service in September 1898. Later, in a letter to sculptor James E. Kelly—who like Frederick MacMonnies sculpted a statuette of the Rough Rider upon a horse—Roosevelt described in detail how he looked and dressed in the war. Unlike his image here, he said, "In Cuba I did not have the side of my hat turned up."

Theodore Roosevelt by an unidentified photographer, platinum print, 28.5 x 23.7 cm. (11⁵⁄₁₆ x 9⁵⁄₁₆ in.), 1898. NATIONAL PORTRAIT GALLERY, SMITHSONIAN INSTITUTION, WASHINGTON, D.C.; GIFT OF JOANNA STURM

Theodore Roosevelt and the Rough Riders at San Juan Heights by William Dinwiddie, (1867–1934), photograph, 17.8 x 25.4 cm. (7 x 10 in.), 1898. THEODORE ROOSEVELT COLLECTION, HARVARD COLLEGE LIBRARY, CAMBRIDGE, MASSACHUSETTS; THEODORE ROOSEVELT ESTATE DEPOSIT. BY PERMISSION OF THE THEODORE ROOSEVELT ASSOCIATION

Where exactly sculptor Frederick MacMonnies had seen a picture of Roosevelt jumping a horse (Jacob Riis published one in his 1904 biography) is not certain. Yet the image impressed him enough that he wanted to use it to model a statuette of Roosevelt in his Rough Rider uniform. Roosevelt was "delighted" (an expression he used frequently) to be the subject of a sculpture by one of the nation's foremost practitioners. He objected, however, to MacMonnies's intention of depicting him in uniform jumping a horse. "I do not jump fences in my khaki and with sword and revolver in my belt," Roosevelt informed the sculptor. "If you want to make me jumping a fence I must send you my ordinary riding things. It seems to me it would be better to put me in khaki and not to have me jumping the fence." As the artist's finished sculpture attests, he ignored Roosevelt's concerns and modeled him as he pleased, heroically in uniform on a leaping steed, and holding his hat in the air. In the spring of 1905, MacMonnies presented this statuette to the President and first lady.

The Rough Rider by Frederick MacMonnies (1863–1937), bronze, 64.8 cm. (25½ in.) height, 1905. Sagamore Hill National Historic Site, National Park Service, Oyster Bay, New York

Fedor Encke's portrait of Roosevelt the Rough Rider was presented to Roosevelt in December 1902 by a close friend and political supporter, Maria Longworth Storer. Mrs. Storer was the aunt of Roosevelt's future son-in-law, Nicholas Longworth. With her husband, Bellamy, she had been friends with the McKinleys; the Storers allegedly were among the party that had recommended Roosevelt for the post of assistant secretary of the navy in 1897. As President, Roosevelt's power and influence grew appreciably, and so too did Mrs. Storer's demands on him. Just months before she presented Encke's portrait, Roosevelt had appointed her husband to be the ambassador to Austria-Hungary, an appointment Roosevelt would rescind in 1906 because of diplomatic embarrassments occasioned by Mrs. Storer. She had a meddlesome disposition and used little discretion. Yet at the time, Roosevelt accepted her gift with genuine appreciation. "I took an immense fancy to the picture," he wrote her. He admitted that he did not think it looked particularly like himself. Nevertheless, "it *does* look the way I should like to have my children and possibly grandchildren *think* that I looked!"

Roosevelt had his new portrait hung in the White House dining room, and a picture of it appeared in *Harper's Weekly* in May 1903. Today the portrait hangs in the landing leading into Roosevelt's grand trophy room in his house at Sagamore Hill.

Theodore Roosevelt by Fedor Encke (born 1851), oil on canvas, 152.4 x 101.6 cm. (60 x 40 in.), 1902. SAGAMORE HILL NATIONAL HISTORIC SITE, NATIONAL PARK SERVICE, OYSTER BAY, NEW YORK

occurred only weeks after he returned from Cuba was but the first political measure of his new military fame. Party leaders saw him as a sterling alternative to the incumbent Republican, Governor Frank S. Black, whose repairs to the Erie Canal had triggered charges of scandal and corruption. Nevertheless, the party boss, United States Senator Thomas C. Platt, was not easily convinced about Roosevelt. Platt was old and feeble, but he was highly skilled at making machine politics work so as not to arouse voter antagonism. For his willingness to compromise, he was called the "Easy Boss." Platt no longer trusted Governor Black, who had become a political liability. He was equally leery of Roosevelt for his independent streak, in spite of TR's professions that he would work with party leaders in all good faith and conscience.

Roosevelt's conscience was what troubled Platt the most. The senator was never one to practice politics by the Good Book. Moreover, said Platt, "If he [TR] becomes Governor of New York, sooner or later, with his personality, he will have to be President of the United States." Platt did not want to be the one "to start that thing going."[11] Assured finally that Roosevelt would be a safe candidate and would not defy the party machine, he reluctantly endorsed him. When a question concerning Roosevelt's legal residency threatened to derail his bid, lawyers and backers successfully argued this to be a technicality and a non-issue. In an election in which the Democrats would have prevailed over any other candidate, Roosevelt won a majority by more than seventeen thousand votes.

The governorship was a two-year office, and after a few short months, Platt realized that he could not control his spirited young lieutenant. From the start, the two leaders were at odds. Roosevelt would not be bullied into making key appointments. His refusal to reappoint Louis F. Payn as the state superintendent of insurance prompted him to quote the West African proverb that the press made famous: "Speak softly and carry a big stick; you will go far."[12] Platt was infuriated at Roosevelt for his support of a franchise bill that would tax public-service corporations. These businesses had relied upon the

As governor of New York, Roosevelt pressed his efforts to bring about honesty and efficiency in government. His successful fight to remove Louis Payn as superintendent of insurance was a victory for him against the powerful machine politicians. Roosevelt accused Payn of selling his political influence to the corporations who were backing the machine. Horace Taylor's cover illustration for the *Verdict* in February 1900 presented a timely interpretation of the Payn episode. Here Taylor adapted the tradition of Groundhog Day, February 2, to depict Louis Payn's fate as he sees the shadow of Theodore Roosevelt. For Payn, now out of a comfortable job, it was "going to be a hard, cold winter!"

The Ground Hog's Shadow by Horace Taylor (1864–1921), chromolithograph, 31.8 x 24.2 cm. (12½ x 9½ in.), for *Verdict*, February 12, 1900. THEODORE ROOSEVELT COLLECTION, HARVARD COLLEGE LIBRARY, CAMBRIDGE, MASSACHUSETTS

President William McKinley (1843–1901) by Frances Benjamin Johnston (1864–1952), platinum print, 20.8 x 14.9 cm. (8⁵⁄₁₆ x 5⅞ in.), circa 1899. NATIONAL PORTRAIT GALLERY, SMITHSONIAN INSTITUTION, WASHINGTON, D.C.

McKinley-Roosevelt umbrella from the campaign of 1900. POLITICAL HISTORY DIVISION, NATIONAL MUSEUM OF AMERICAN HISTORY, SMITHSONIAN INSTITUTION, WASHINGTON, D.C.

senator's protection. Now they leaned upon him to somehow oust the governor. By February 1900, a desperate Platt was supporting the idea of Roosevelt running as William McKinley's Vice President in the fall election. The recent death of Vice President Garret A. Hobart had left a vacancy for which

In this cartoon for *Judge,* Grant Hamilton illustrated Roosevelt's popularity as a war hero, and accurately predicted his ultimate political destiny, the White House.

Is It Only Shadow? by Grant Hamilton (circa 1862–1920), hand-colored lithographic proof, 27.7 x 43.2 cm. (10⅞ x 17 in.), for *Judge,* October 29, 1898. Theodore Roosevelt Birthplace National Historic Site, National Park Service, New York City

"I am a comparatively young man yet and I like to work. I do not like to be a figurehead."

The Glad Hand by R. L. Bristol; see page 21.

many thought Roosevelt was a perfect choice, partly because there was no one else. Roosevelt understood the futility of the office. "In the Vice Presidency I could do nothing," he wrote to Henry Cabot Lodge. "I am a comparatively young man yet and I like to work. I do not like to be a figurehead."[15]

With the prospects of TR being a factor in the presidential contest, the nation's comic illustrators explored all of the nuances of political hyperbole. The Rough Rider was a natural for caricature, and inspired cartoons by the hundreds. The face-off between the governor and the senator was illustrated masterfully on the cover of *Verdict* on April 16, 1900, the day before the New York state convention elected Roosevelt to be a delegate-at-large to the Republican National Convention. Drawn by R. L. Bristol and titled *The Glad Hand*, the cartoon depicts a bespectacled Roosevelt and a bearded Platt shaking hands and smiling, face-to-face. Each holds a pointed sword behind his back, however. Illuminating the governor's chair hangs a shining lamp labeled "NY State Convention." The caption predicts, "Wait til the light is turned out and the air will be full of eye-glasses and pointed whiskers."

For Platt, the governor's chair was the only issue. He wielded the bigger blade and had the political power to deny Roosevelt's renomination. In June at the Philadelphia convention, TR could not help being his ebullient self. He made himself conspicuous in a dark slouch hat, reminiscent of the ones his Rough Riders had worn; he enjoyed being the center of national attention, no matter how much he protested his almost unanimous nomination to be President McKinley's vice-presidential running mate. Roosevelt dutifully accepted, much to the dismay of Ohio Senator Marcus A. Hanna, chairman of the national Republican committee. Hanna, an old friend of McKinley and his political adviser, was a self-proclaimed champion of the status quo, a friend to big business and organized capital. Roosevelt's reputation as a reformer scared him. In addition, he feared that his popularity would only undermine that of the President, whose image bore all the gravity of an undertaker's. For Hanna, the cartoons showing a dwarfed McKinley riding on the pommel of TR's saddle, and of the giant shadow of Roosevelt the Rough Rider

The Supreme Moment. Chief Justice Fuller
Administering the Oath of Office to
President William McKinley, March 4, 1901
by Underwood and Underwood (active
1882–circa 1950), albumen silver print,
stereo view, 8 x 15.5 cm. (3 5/16 x 6 1/8 in.),
1901. NATIONAL PORTRAIT GALLERY,
SMITHSONIAN INSTITUTION, WASHINGTON, D.C.

encroaching across the lawn of the White House, were all too real. Hanna pondered the unthinkable—What if McKinley should die in office? These were his worries throughout the campaign, and McKinley's election that fall only aggravated them, for TR—the new vice president elect—was suddenly "one life" away from becoming President of the United States.

1. Morris, *Roosevelt*, pp. 161–62.

2. Ibid., pp. 162–63.

3. Roosevelt to Lodge, May 5, 1884, *The Letters of Theodore Roosevelt*, ed. Elting E. Morison (Cambridge, Mass., 1951–1954), vol. 1, p. 69; Pringle, *Roosevelt*, pp. 92–93; Roosevelt, *Autobiography*, p. 100.

4. Pringle, *Roosevelt*, p. 97; Roosevelt to Lodge, August 12, 1884, *Letters*, vol. 1, p. 77.

5. Roosevelt to Lodge, June 29, 1889, *Letters*, vol. 1, p. 167.

6. Pringle, *Roosevelt*, p. 139.

7. Ibid., p. 171.

8. Roosevelt to John Moore, April 28, 1898, Roosevelt to Brooks Brothers, May 2, 1898, Roosevelt to William Wingate Sewall, May 4, 1898, *Letters*, vol. 2, pp. 821–23; Morris, *Roosevelt*, p. 612.

9. Pringle, *Roosevelt*, p. 181.

10. Ibid., pp. 197–98.

11. Miller, *Roosevelt*, p. 311.

12. Roosevelt to Henry L. Sprague, January 26, 1900, *Letters*, vol. 2, p. 1141.

13. Roosevelt to Lodge, February 2, 1900, ibid., p. 1161.

Captions:
Page 26: "It is I think," Roosevelt to Caspar Whitney, March 16, 1901, *Letters*, vol. 3, p. 16. *Page 28*: "I do not believe," Roosevelt, *Autobiography*, p. 96. *Page 29:* "I wish I were with you," Roosevelt to Remington, September 15, 1897, *Letters*, vol. 1, p. 680. *Page 38*: "In Cuba I did not," Roosevelt to James Edward Kelley, May 6, 1901, *Letters*, vol. 3, p. 71. *Page 40*: "I do not jump fences," Roosevelt to MacMonnies, November 19, 1904, *Letters*, vol. 4, p. 1035. *Page 41*: "I took an immense fancy," Roosevelt to Maria Longworth Storer, December 8, 1902, *Letters*, vol. 3, p. 391.

Chapter 2

Rough Rider in the White House

THEODORE ROOSEVELT had presidential ambitions as much as anyone in the country, but he never shared Senator Hanna's anxiety about his ever having to take that oath of office in an emergency. Roosevelt's official duties as Vice President consisted solely of presiding over the Senate, and this lasted for only four days in March 1901. After Congress adjourned until December, Roosevelt contemplated again studying law to help fill his days with structured activity. Privately he complained that the office of the Vice President should be abolished.

On September 6, 1901, Roosevelt was attending a meeting of the Vermont Fish and Game League on the Isle La Motte on Lake Champlain, when he received a telephone call alerting him that President McKinley had been shot by a young anarchist in Buffalo. He hurried to the scene and remained in the city several days, until McKinley's condition improved. Confident that the President would recover and to reassure the public, Roosevelt joined his family vacationing at Camp Tahawus, a remote region of the Adirondack Mountains. On Friday, the thirteenth, he was descending the slopes of Mount Marcy, the highest peak in the state of New York, when a messenger emerged from the mist with a telegram—McKinley was dying! Roosevelt again hastened to Buffalo, arriving nearly twelve hours after McKinley had died, the third President to be assassinated. In what is now a national historic site, Roosevelt took the oath of office in the home of Ansley Wilcox, a prominent lawyer and civic leader. Six weeks shy of his

At the invitation of the first family, John Singer Sargent was a White House guest for a week in the middle of February 1903, while he painted a portrait of the President. For Sargent, the foremost Anglo-American portraitist of his era, the experience was vexing in many respects. Particularly, Sargent found the President's strong will daunting from the start. The choice of a suitable place to paint, where the lighting was good, tried Roosevelt's patience. No room on the first floor agreed with the artist. When they began climbing the staircase, Roosevelt told Sargent he did not think the artist knew what he wanted. Sargent replied that he did not think Roosevelt knew what was involved in posing for a portrait. Roosevelt, who had just reached the landing, swung around, placing his hand on the newel and said, "Don't I!"

forty-third birthday, he became the youngest President of the United States before or since.

No event had a more profound effect on Theodore Roosevelt's political career than the death of William McKinley. Recently he had written to his friend, the New York City reformer Jacob Riis, that "a shadow" had fallen across his path, separating him forever from the days of his youth. Roosevelt, however, refused to be morbid about his own destiny.[1] The job at hand was too big to worry about, and finding solutions to the domestic and international issues that were affecting the lives of Americans would take all of his enormous energy. From the start, he was committed to making the government work for the people, and in many respects, the people never needed government more. The post–Civil War industrial revolution had generated great wealth and power for the men who controlled the levers of business and capital. Regulating the great business trusts to foster fair competition without socializing the free enterprise system would be one of Roosevelt's primary concerns. The railroads, labor, and the processed food industry all came under his scrutiny. Although the regulations he implemented were modest by today's standards, collectively they were a significant first step in an age before warning labels and consumer lawsuits.

Internationally, America was on the threshold of world leadership. Acquisition of the Philippines and Guam after the recent war with Spain expanded the nation's territorial borders almost to Asia. The Panama Canal would only increase American trade and defense interests in the Far East, as well as in Central and South America. In an age that saw the rise of oceanic steamship travel, the country's sense of isolation was on the verge of suddenly becoming as antiquated as yardarms and sails.

A conservative by nature, Roosevelt was progressive in the way he addressed the nation's problems and modern in his view of the presidency. If the people were to be served, according to him, then it was incumbent upon the President to orchestrate the initiatives that would be to their benefit and the nation's welfare. Not since Abraham Lincoln, and Andrew Jackson before him, had a President exercised his executive

Sargent saw his opportunity and told the President not to move; this would be the pose and the location for the sittings. Still, over the next few days Sargent was frustrated by the President's busy schedule, which limited their sessions to a half-hour after lunch. Sargent would have liked to have had more time. Nevertheless, Roosevelt considered the portrait a complete success. He liked it immensely, and continued to favor it for the rest of his life. Commissioned by the federal government, Sargent's *Roosevelt* is the official White House portrait of the twenty-sixth President.

Theodore Roosevelt by John Singer Sargent (1856–1925), oil on canvas, 147.6 x 101.6 cm. (58⅛ x 40 in.), 1903. THE WHITE HOUSE, WASHINGTON, D.C.

Theodore Roosevelt was hurrying to the
city of Buffalo, where he would take the
oath of office to become the twenty-sixth
President, when this issue of the *Buffalo
Courier* appeared just after the death of
President William McKinley.

Buffalo Courier, September 14, 1901.
THEODORE ROOSEVELT INAUGURAL SITE
FOUNDATION, BUFFALO, NEW YORK

*"Is there any law that
will prevent me from
declaring Pelican
Island a Federal Bird
Reservation? . . . Very
well, then I so declare
it!"*

powers as an equal branch of government. If the Constitution
did not specifically deny the President the exercise of power,
Roosevelt felt at liberty to do so. "Is there any law that will prevent me from declaring Pelican Island a Federal Bird
Reservation? . . . Very well, then I so declare it!" By executive

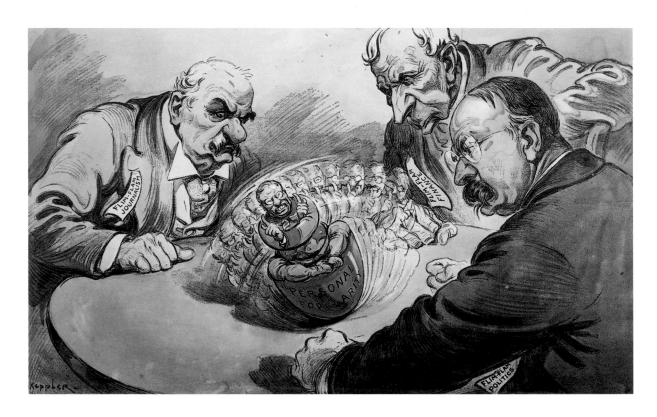

President Roosevelt's mandate to regulate big business won wide approval with the electorate. In this *Puck* cartoon, three of the country's most powerful business-men—*(left to right)* J. Pierpont Morgan, John D. Rockefeller, and Edward H. Harriman, chief executive of the Union Pacific Railroad—watch with frustrated wonder at the buoyancy of Roosevelt's "Personal Popularity."

He Bobs Up Serenely by Udo J. Keppler (1872–1956), hand-colored lithographic proof, 36.2 x 53.3 cm. (14¼ x 21 in.), for *Puck*, October 9, 1907. THEODORE ROOSEVELT BIRTHPLACE NATIONAL HISTORIC SITE, NATIONAL PARK SERVICE, NEW YORK CITY

☛

J. Pierpont Morgan (1837–1913) was the dean of American financiers at the start of the twentieth century. His banking empire, J. P. Morgan & Company, had either controlling or financial interests in several major railroads and industries, including United States Steel, International Harvester, General Electric, and American Telephone & Telegraph. Morgan not only kept his finger on the pulse of American business, but a directive from his desk in Manhattan could influence the stock market itself, which happened in the panic of 1907, when he lent his prestige and collateral to help stabilize Wall Street. Morgan's special gift was for consolidating businesses so that they might be more efficient and profitable. In the interests of the public, and through government regulation, Roosevelt sought to curtail the monopolistic power of the big trusts, and not necessarily to break them.

J. Pierpont Morgan by Adrian Lamb (1901–1988), after the 1888 oil by Frank Holl, oil on canvas, 127 x 102.2 cm. (50 x 40¼ in.), 1966. NATIONAL PORTRAIT GALLERY, SMITHSONIAN INSTITUTION, WASHINGTON, D.C.; GIFT OF H. S. MORGAN

order in March 1903, he established the first of fifty-one national bird sanctuaries. These and the national parks he created are a part of his great legacy. But at the time, critics viewed such action as tyrannical. "Almost every week his Administration has been characterized by some outrageous act of usurpation," wrote one angry newspaper editor; "he is the most dangerous foe to human liberty that has ever set foot on American soil." Roosevelt clearly understood he was treading on new ground. "I did not usurp power," he explained in his *Autobiography*, "but I did greatly broaden the use of executive power. . . . I acted for the common well-being of all our people."[2]

Roosevelt understood, too, that if he did not take action at certain times, the people would become the trodden. The Pennsylvania coal miners' strike of 1902 was an unprecedented example. Roosevelt had no constitutional authority to intervene in the dispute between the striking miners and the mine operators. Yet the approach of winter and the prospects of Americans growing cold and hungry for want of fuel compelled him to bring the two sides together, or else send federal troops in to operate the anthracite mines. Roosevelt's perseverance and threats loosened the grip of the operators, and the strikers went back to work with a new contract.

That Roosevelt was right for the times was evident in the business attitude of Wall Street mega-financier J. Pierpont Morgan. After Roosevelt ordered an antitrust suit filed against the Northern Securities Company, a railroad trust in which Morgan had a controlling interest, Morgan hurried to the White House to try and resolve the matter in a gentlemanly manner. "If we have done anything wrong, send your man to my man and they can fix it up," he suggested. Impossible, said Roosevelt. The government was not in a position to bargain. In 1904, the Supreme Court found the giant railroad monopoly to be in violation of the Sherman Antitrust Act of 1890 and ordered it dissolved.[3] In this and other antitrust suits, TR put teeth into what heretofore had been a lame act. Roosevelt's initial challenge to big business, the financial lifeline of the Republican Party, went against Senator Hanna's advice to the

"I did not usurp power," he explained in his Autobiography, "but I did greatly broaden the use of executive power. . . . I acted for the common well-being of all our people."

Cecilia Beaux made this drawing of President Roosevelt in April 1902, at the time of a White House debut of her oil portrait of Mrs. Roosevelt with her daughter, Ethel. Beaux later commented on her portrait of the President: "It's just a head, but I don't believe more of the figure would add to its interest. He sat for about two hours—talking and reading Kipling, reciting the same, also Browning and was most loveable and delicious."

Theodore Roosevelt by Cecilia Beaux (1855–1942), charcoal on paper, 45.4 x 35.3 cm. (17⅞ x 13⅞ in.), 1902. MUSEUM OF AMERICAN ART OF THE PENNSYLVANIA ACADEMY OF THE FINE ARTS, PHILADELPHIA; GIFT OF HENRY SANDWITH DRINKER

young, inexperienced President—to proceed slowly in his new and high office. Roosevelt announced emphatically that he intended to continue William McKinley's policies for peace and prosperity, and cartoons depicted him taking a seat at McKinley's desk, his Rough Rider uniform and sword hanging on a coat-hook behind him. Still, Roosevelt was Roosevelt. Inactivity was anathema to his personality and inconsistent with his reputation as a reformer in every previous job he had

Peter Juley's photograph of President Roosevelt dressed in his riding clothes appeared on the cover of *Harper's Weekly*, July 2, 1904.

Theodore Roosevelt by Peter A. Juley (1862–1937), gelatin silver print, 50 x 37.8 cm. (19¹¹⁄₁₆ x 14⅞ in.), 1903. National Portrait Gallery, Smithsonian Institution, Washington, D.C.; gift of Joanna Sturm

His famous "Tennis Cabinet" was indicative of how he liked to work. Riding and hiking were almost daily pastimes; one senator joked that anyone wishing to have any influence with the President would have to buy a horse.

held. In waiting six months before pressing suit against the Northern Securities Company, he had demonstrated reasonable restraint by his standards.

TR's dynamic view of the presidency infused vigor into a branch of government that traditionally had been ceremonial and sedate. His famous "Tennis Cabinet" was indicative of how he liked to work. Riding and hiking were almost daily pastimes; one senator joked that anyone wishing to have any influence with the President would have to buy a horse. Especially invigorating were his point-to-point walks in Rock Creek Park. The rule was over rocks and through creeks, never around obstacles. As the French ambassador once discovered, accompanying Roosevelt on one of his outings might require wading naked through deep water, with the Frenchman wearing only kid gloves, in deference to any ladies who might happen upon the scene unawares. When the press could keep pace with him, it reveled in his activities, making him the first celebrity of the twentieth century. His toothy image adorned countless magazine covers before beauty, sex, and scandal became chic. Photographers captured the animated Roosevelt jumping horses, chopping wood, and giving speeches, his hands waving like a symphony conductor, whereas painters and sculptors preserved, more or less, a measure of his formal dignity for posterity. And seemingly everywhere Roosevelt was leaping off cartoonists' drawing boards.

Like Roosevelt himself, the first family was young, energetic, and a novelty in the White House. Public interest in them was spontaneous. Pictures of Theodore, Edith, and their six children began appearing in newspapers before Roosevelt reached Buffalo to take the oath of office. Ages of the two girls and four boys ranged from Alice, age seventeen, to Quentin, age six. For once in its history, the executive mansion acquired aspects of a normal American home, complete with roller skates, bicycles, and tennis rackets. The furnishings and art would suffer a few indignities, such as the time when Quentin and his chums pelted the portraits with spitballs. Yet overall, the Roosevelts made improvements to what had become a staid house, filled with tired and pompous Victorian

Copyright
PACK BROS
1903

ROOSEVELT & FAMILY 1903

The Roosevelt family (left to right): Quentin (1897–1918), Theodore (1858–1919), Theodore Jr. (1887–1944), Archibald (1894–1979), Alice Lee (1884–1980), Kermit (1889–1943), Edith Kermit (1861–1948), and Ethel Carow (1891–1977) by Pach Brothers studio (active since 1867), gelatin silver print, 24.1 x 31.8 cm. (9½ x 12½ in.), 1903. THEODORE ROOSEVELT COLLECTION, HARVARD COLLEGE LIBRARY, CAMBRIDGE, MASSACHUSSETTS

First Lady Edith Kermit Roosevelt had a classical profile, as recorded here by photographer J. Schloss in 1901. (A similar profile view was allegedly her husband's favorite picture of her.) Schloss's image appeared in *Harper's Weekly*, January 18, 1902. "Under her leadership," reported *Harper's*, "the social life of the White House has been broadened and brightened as it has not been since the days of Dolley Madison."

Edith Kermit Roosevelt by J. Schloss (lifedates unknown), photograph, 27.9 x 19.1 cm. (11 x 7½ in.), 1901. THEODORE ROOSEVELT COLLECTION, HARVARD COLLEGE LIBRARY, CAMBRIDGE, MASSACHUSETTS

furnishings. As part of a general restoration, they redecorated in a more authentic classical style. Since the eve of the Jacksonian era, the executive mansion had been referred to as the White House. In 1901, Roosevelt made that designation official.

As first lady, Edith was the first to hire a social secretary. She also began the White House china collection and the series of first ladies' portraits. Unlike her husband, who used his high office as a "bully pulpit" to espouse opinions on everything from the advantages of simplified spelling to the fraudulence of the "nature-fakers" (nature writers who were exaggerating the intelligence of wildlife), Edith instilled a sense of formal dignity to official functions. Rarely before had protocol been more rigidly observed. State dinners were now elegant affairs with trumpet calls and catered food, a vast improvement over any fare the house chefs could concoct. In all that was domestic, Edith was indisputably head of the Roosevelt household. Although not domineering, she, like her husband, had decided opinions about her domain, which of course included the rearing of six children. Nothing was ever done on their behalf without her approval. Not infrequently she looked upon her husband as a seventh child. His impulses were such that during one outing, he let the children go swimming in their clothes rather than deny them the opportunity because they had no bathing suits. "You must always remember," wrote Cecil Spring-Rice in 1904, "that the President is about six."[4]

Roosevelt's eldest child, Alice, was an impressionable teenager when he became President. High-spirited and defiant by nature, she enjoyed pushing the limits of decorum, while competing for her father's attention. Naturally she was a favorite of the press, which called her Princess Alice. Stories about her antics, her favorite color, a blue-gray dubbed "Alice blue," and her cast of acquaintances filled the newspapers. She smoked in public, bet at the racetrack, and was caught speeding in her red runabout by the Washington police. Photographs of her connote the classic Gibson Girl and suggest an air of youthful haughtiness. Gentlemen found her wit enticing. At her White House debut in 1902, her charms kept them "seven deep around her all the time." She complained about the punch, wanted champagne instead, but still "had the time of her life." In 1906, she married Nicholas Longworth, a Republican congressman from Ohio. He was fifteen years her senior, short and bald, and something of a bon vivant. The President looked upon the groom, the son of a wealthy Cincinnati family with a promising career in politics, as a good prospect for his daughter. Edith, however, always the better judge of character, was leery about his drinking habits. But no

As a former presiding officer of the United States Senate, Roosevelt was requested by that body to sit for a sculpted bust in 1904. His first choice of an artist was Augustus Saint-Gaudens, but he declined because of ill health. In his place, he recommended his former assistant, James Earle Fraser, whom Roosevelt accepted as a worthy substitute. The sittings took place in the East Room of the White House in the early mornings and again late in the afternoons. Roosevelt stated exactly how he wished to be modeled, without his spectacles and with his head thrown back. Fraser, however, soon discovered that Roosevelt's expression would be truer to life if he would wear his glasses, to which the President complied. Impressed by the forceful way in which Roosevelt leaned his head forward to make a point, Fraser next wanted to sculpt his subject in such a pose. "By George, that *is* good!" exclaimed the President when he saw the altered clay model. The Senate, however, rejected this bust, because it depicted Roosevelt dressed in his Rough Rider attire. Fraser did a second, less successful, bust in marble for the Senate; he modeled Roosevelt according to his original wishes, and attired him in a Prince Albert coat. The bronze cast shown here was made in 1920, and preserves the spontaneity and vigor of Fraser's original interpretation.

Theodore Roosevelt by James Earle Fraser (1876–1953), bronze, 23.5 cm. (9¼ in.) height, 1920. NATIONAL PORTRAIT GALLERY, SMITHSONIAN INSTITUTION, WASHINGTON, D.C.

Alice Lee Roosevelt and Nicholas
Longworth (1869–1931) on their wedding
day, with the President by Edward S.
Curtis (1868–1952), photograph, 1906.
PRINTS AND PHOTOGRAPHS DIVISION, LIBRARY OF
CONGRESS, WASHINGTON, D.C.

*At her White House
debut in 1902, her
charms kept them "seven
deep around her all the
time." She complained
about the punch,
wanted champagne
instead, but still "had
the time of her life."*

one could deny that Alice was genuinely in love. Her White
House wedding in February 1906 was the most talked-about
social event of the Roosevelt years.[5]

In matters affecting the nation, Roosevelt's campaign to
regulate big business preoccupied his administration from

Edward S. Curtis made this photograph of President Roosevelt in 1904, three years before he published the first volume of his monumental twenty-volume study, *The North American Indian.* In more than forty thousand photographs, Curtis documented the life of the Indians as a way of preserving their vanishing culture. In a foreword for volume one, Roosevelt wrote of his friend Curtis, "He is an artist who works out of doors and not in the closet." In February 1906, Curtis was invited to be the official photographer at Alice Lee Roosevelt's wedding. This image of the President was published in a special July 1905 issue of *McClure's* magazine devoted to members of the first family.

Theodore Roosevelt by Edward S. Curtis (1868–1952), platinum print, 39.8 x 30.2 cm. (15¹¹/₁₆ x 11⅞ in.), 1904. NATIONAL PORTRAIT GALLERY, SMITHSONIAN INSTITUTION, WASHINGTON, D.C.

beginning to end, earning him the sobriquet of the "Trust Buster." The Elkins Act of 1903 and the tougher Hepburn Act of 1906 banned the practice of the railroads giving rebates to preferred shippers. John D. Rockefeller's Standard Oil Company was the most notorious setter of special rates. A

A Tip to Fatima Ted by Udo J. Keppler (1872–1956), hand-colored lithographic proof, 33 x 25.4 cm. (13 x 10 in.), for *Puck,* August 15, 1906. THEODORE ROOSEVELT BIRTHPLACE NATIONAL HISTORIC SITE, NATIONAL PARK SERVICE, NEW YORK CITY

Irving Ramsay Wiles's career as a society painter followed on the heels of the great John Singer Sargent. His portrait of actress Julia Marlowe was a sensation at a National Academy of Design exhibition in 1902, and virtually established his reputation for capturing the essence of his sitters with dazzling brushwork. His portraits of men tended to be more subdued, as was the case with his portrait of President Roosevelt. Wiles painted the original canvas in 1906 and sent it to the University of Berlin, where a chair in history had just been established in Roosevelt's name. The portrait was destroyed in World War II. Wiles also painted the copy portrait shown here that same year.

Theodore Roosevelt by Irving Ramsay Wiles (1861–1948), oil on canvas, 171.5 x 97.8 cm. (67½ x 38½ in.), 1906. THEODORE ROOSEVELT BIRTHPLACE NATIONAL HISTORIC SITE, NATIONAL PARK SERVICE, NEW YORK CITY

report released in March 1906 by Roosevelt's newly established Bureau of Corporations charged that Standard was making three-quarters of a million dollars annually in illegal profits. The public at large supported the administration's tough new edicts, as illustrated in a cartoon by Homer Davenport for the *New York Evening Mail.* Davenport depicted a determined-looking Roosevelt standing with his foot on the head of a prostrate man, identified by his hat as a "Rebater." In the background, Davenport illustrated the public's approval with applauding hands and hats tossed in the air. At Roosevelt's feet lie a brick labeled "From a Certain Corporation" and a rock labeled "From a Trust." These are allusions to Standard Oil and to J. Pierpont Morgan's dissolved trust, the Northern Securities Company.

Earlier, when Davenport had been drawing for William Randolph Hearst's *New York Journal,* he had been critical of Roosevelt and the Republicans. State party boss Tom Platt at one point tried unsuccessfully to stop Davenport's barbs by trying to pass an anti-cartoon bill. The artist, however, came to admire Roosevelt's policies and switched to the Republican *Mail* in 1904. That year he produced a cartoon of Uncle Sam standing behind Roosevelt with the caption "He's good enough for me." This popular image was put on buttons and posters, and became the most widely circulated campaign document of the 1904 election. Although simple in design, the drawing underscored the technical deficiencies in most of Davenport's work. He never quite mastered human anatomy. His "Rebater" cartoon, based on the popular 1904 campaign drawing, is one of his better efforts. Roosevelt's arms and legs are anatomically correct, neither too long or too short, and his profile is exceptionally lifelike.

To help persuade standpat Republican senators to pass legislation regulating interstate commerce, Roosevelt began talking softly about lowering the protective tariff. This was a political fireball that not even Roosevelt wanted to touch with a big stick. For the August 15, 1906, cover of *Puck,* Udo J. Keppler illustrated the reaction of big business. He was

"Roosevelt Standing on a Rebater" by Homer C. Davenport (1867–1912), pen and ink, 62.2 x 44.5 cm. (24½ x 17½ in.), not dated. THEODORE ROOSEVELT BIRTHPLACE NATIONAL HISTORIC SITE, NATIONAL PARK SERVICE, NEW YORK CITY

inspired by Charles Perrault's seventeenth-century fairy tale about Bluebeard, a murderous husband who gave his wife, Fatima, all the keys to the castle save one—the key to the chamber wherein lay the bodies of his former wives. In Keppler's interpretation, Bluebeard, representing "Protected Monopolies," holds a handful of keys labeled "rate regulation," "meat inspection," "pure food," and "anti-trust laws." He warns Fatima Ted, "With these keys, my dear, you may go as far as you like, but don't let me catch you in *that* room!" The forbidden door is "Tariff Revision."

When it came to reform politics, Roosevelt's progressivism was right down the middle of the road. He lambasted the "malefactors of great wealth" for their abusive business practices, as well as the muckraking journalists, who were reporting only the most dire aspects of American free enterprise.[6] The evil on one side was corporate greed, and on the other socialistic agitation. Somewhere between, he thought, lay the interests of the vast majority of Americans, who would benefit directly from pure food and drug laws and meat inspection standards, all enacted in 1906.

Before the railroads, the mine operators, and the lumber companies had done irreversible damage to the country's seemingly endless natural wealth and resources, Roosevelt used his presidential authority directly. By executive order he established four game preserves, five national parks, fifty-one bird reservations, and one hundred fifty national forests. He designated eighteen national monuments, including the Grand Canyon. In 1904, he signed legislation creating the United States Forest Service and selected Gifford Pinchot as its head. Four years later, he convened at the White House the first conference of governors to address the conservation of natural resources.

At the Isthmus of Panama, Theodore Roosevelt contemplated another kind of national monument, not to be preserved, but to be developed for the benefit of the United States, as well as the international community. The idea of building a canal through the tropical narrows of Central America, there-

President Roosevelt poses with naturalist John Muir on Overhanging Rock, Glacier Point, during a four-day camping trip in Yosemite, California, in May 1903.

Theodore Roosevelt and John Muir by an unidentified photographer, gelatin silver print, 61 x 47 cm. (24 x 18½ in.), 1903. THEODORE ROOSEVELT COLLECTION, HARVARD COLLEGE LIBRARY, CAMBRIDGE, MASSACHUSETTS

☛

On an extended visit to the West in the spring of 1903, Roosevelt sought the company of naturalists John Burroughs and John Muir. With Burroughs, Roosevelt camped in Yellowstone Park for two weeks, and with Muir he explored the wonders of the Yosemite Valley and had his picture taken in front of a giant sequoia tree in the Mariposa Grove. Roosevelt's visit was an opportunity for Muir to be able to impress upon the President the need for immediate preservation measures, especially for the giant forests. In 1908, Roosevelt paid tribute to Muir by designating Muir Woods—a redwood forest north of San Francisco—a national monument.

John Muir (1838–1914) by Orlando Rouland (1871–1945), oil on canvas, 92.1 x 71.8 cm. (36¼ x 28¼ in.), not dated. NATIONAL PORTRAIT GALLERY, SMITHSONIAN INSTITUTION, WASHINGTON, D.C.; GIFT OF MRS. E. H. HARRIMAN TO THE UNITED STATES NATIONAL MUSEUM, 1920

by connecting the Atlantic and Pacific oceans, was an old one. Roosevelt seized upon it as a means of improving the nation's trade and defense capacities. "To my mind," he wrote in 1903, "this building of the canal through Panama will rank in kind, though not of course in degree, with the Louisiana Purchase and the acquisition of Texas."[7]

The President and Mrs. Roosevelt arrived in Cristobal, Panama, on November 17, 1906, during a tour to inspect construction of the canal. This photograph appeared in *Harper's Weekly* on December 8, 1906.

President Roosevelt and Mrs. Roosevelt Landing at Cristobal by Underwood and Underwood (active 1882–circa 1950), brown-toned gelatin silver print, 25.4 x 20.4 cm. (10 x 8 in.), 1906. NATIONAL PORTRAIT GALLERY, SMITHSONIAN INSTITUTION, WASHINGTON, D.C.; GIFT OF JOANNA STURM

In cartoons for the *New York Herald* and *Harper's Weekly*, William A. Rogers criticized Roosevelt's Panama Canal Treaty. None, however, was more poignant than *The News Reaches Bogotá*, which appeared in the *Herald* on November 15, 1903, three days before the Roosevelt administration signed the treaty. In 1922, Rogers published this same cartoon, retitled *The First Spadeful*, in a book of reminiscences, *A World Worth While: A Record of "Auld Acquaintance."*

The News Reaches Bogotá or *The First Spadeful* by William A. Rogers (1854–1931), pen and ink, 43.5 x 53.3 cm. (17⅛ x 21 in.), 1903. PRINTS AND PHOTOGRAPHS DIVISION, LIBRARY OF CONGRESS, WASHINGTON, D.C.

Roosevelt considered the Panama Canal Treaty to have been one of his great accomplishments as President. It was also the most controversial, and the one about which he was the most defensive for the rest of his life. Critics charged that Roosevelt stole the right of way from the Colombian government, which controlled Panama; Roosevelt claimed that he merely took advantage of the revolutionary fervor of the Panamanians. In August 1903, the Colombians rejected an American offer of $10 million for the rights to the Canal Zone, holding out for a better offer. Two months later, the Panamanians staged one of their frequent revolts. On this particular occasion, Roosevelt sent in the United States Navy to dissuade the Colombians from retaliating. He recognized the new government of Panama three days after their successful uprising and promptly negotiated with it the canal treaty that the Colombians had rejected. To the charges that he had fomented the revolution, Roosevelt answered that the Isthmus had been seething with revolution, on which he had kept his foot down while President. This time, "I simply lifted my foot."[8]

Roosevelt's mediation of the Russo-Japanese peace in 1905 is celebrated in this banner depicting the Russian (left) and the Japanese chief negotiators, Count Serge Witte and Baron Jutaro Komura.

Treaty of Portsmouth banner, cotton, 55.9 x 57.2 cm. (22 x 22½ in.), circa 1905. THEODORE ROOSEVELT BIRTHPLACE NATIONAL HISTORIC SITE, NATIONAL PARK SERVICE, NEW YORK CITY

The Warning, a cartoon by Eugene Zimmerman for the cover of the January 19, 1907, issue of *Judge,* concerned President Roosevelt's summary dismissal of 167 soldiers belonging to the United States Army's Twenty-fifth Infantry, an all-black unit stationed in Brownsville, Texas, in 1906. Alleged eyewitnesses in the racially charged town had accused several soldiers of a random shooting spree one August night, which had left one man dead. After a military inquiry failed to produce conclusive evidence of guilt, Roosevelt took the drastic measure of dishonorably discharging the entire regiment, when not a single soldier would volunteer information against any of his fellow enlisted men. Roosevelt was convinced about the guilt of the soldiers, and nothing short of hard evidence to the contrary could make him change his mind—not even politics as the insert to this cartoon suggests: "Watch the Blackman's vote in 1908."

The Warning by Eugene Zimmerman (1862–1935), chromolithograph, 35.6 x 25.4 cm. (14 x 10 in.), for *Judge,* January 19, 1907. THEODORE ROOSEVELT INAUGURAL SITE FOUNDATION, BUFFALO, NEW YORK

THE WARNING.

Roosevelt's Hostility to the Colored People of the United States

THE RECORD OF THE DISCHARGE OF THE COLORED SOLDIERS AT BROWNSVILLE

"It is becoming more and more apparent to me every day, from one official utterance and then another, that President Roosevelt and his associates are prejudiced against the negro and have no real love for him."—W. Calvin Chase, editor of the Washington Bee.

"That President Roosevelt is tinctured with colorphobia is as plain as anything can be."—The Baltimore Afro-American Ledger.

"President Roosevelt is fair in speech in holding out the door of hope to us but in practice we find him false."—The Philadelphia Tribune.

"The one man our race has loved best since Lincoln has betrayed us."—Resolution adopted by the regular Colored Republican Organization of the Ninth New York Assembly District.

"Beyond the shadow of a doubt, Roosevelt has deserted the colored man completely."—J. Douglas Wetmore, of New York City.

The greatest injustice ever done to the colored race in the United States was committed by Theodore Roosevelt when he was President.

By an executive order dated November 5, 1906, Theodore Roosevelt summarily dismissed without honor 170 colored men, enlisted soldiers of the United States, members of Companies B, C, and D, Twenty-fifth Infantry, stationed at Brownsville, Texas. He took this action upon prejudiced statements that the men had been concerned in an affray, and without consultation with the Secretary of War, William H. Taft; without substantial evidence of their guilt, and without giving the accused an opportunity to be heard, Mr. Roosevelt arbitrarily ordered their dismissal in disgrace from the army. Against this order, William H. Taft, unasked, made his protest and actually held up the order of the President at the peril of losing his own job, in order that Mr. Roosevelt might reconsider his decision. This Theodore Roosevelt refused to do and the dismissal followed.

The episode presents a striking example of Theodore Roosevelt's hostility to the colored race. If he had not been carried away by his anti-negro prejudices he never would have committed such an unprecedented and cruel act.

The story of Brownsville and of the storm of universal and emphatic protest which broke around Roosevelt's head should not be forgotten. The affair happened six years ago, and Mr. Roosevelt has done so many things since then that he has successfully diverted attention from this dark page in his official record. He does not, apparently, wish it to be recalled. When he is appealing for the votes of the colored man he carefully refrains from mentioning Brownsville. It is worth while, however, now that he is seeking renomination, regardless of his pledges and promises and in violation of every principle of justice and fair play, to recall the details of an event that at the time of its occurrence profoundly stirred the righteous indignation of every fair-minded and patriotic citizen.

In the month of August, 1906, the three companies mentioned, belonging to the Twenty-fifth Infantry, a regiment of colored soldiers which had a splendid record for discipline and bravery, were stationed at Brownsville, Texas, with white officers in command. They were not wanted by the citizens of the town. Every effort was made to prevent the detail from going into effect. Upon arriving, however, the men acted with great self-restraint. Even upon paydays they were not drunk or disorderly. They had given no occasion for the stories which were current that they were to be the victims

of the anger and hatred of the Brownsville people.

Sometime about midnight on the night of August 13, 1906, there was considerable shooting. The evidence all went to show that the first shots fired were from pistols, although the enlisted men were not equipped with this character of weapon. In the melee a bartender was killed in a saloon and a lieutenant of police was wounded. The colored soldiers, whose presence had always been objectionable to the Texans, were immediately charged with being the authors of the disturbance. This was evidently part of a pre-arranged programme. "The whole affair," wrote a correspondent of the New York Evening Post, "appears to be a miserable outgrowth of race hatred and mob violence on the part of the people of Brownsville."

The white population quickly managed to get its side of the case before President Roosevelt, who accepted the prejudiced and unsubstantiated stories with remarkable promptness. He at once jumped to the conclusion that the soldiers were guilty because the white people said that they were and he demanded that they surrender their alleged guilty comrades. When they declared that they were all innocent, Mr. Roosevelt charged them with maintaining what he called "a conspiracy of silence" and upon this charge arbitrarily dishonorably discharged every enlisted man in the three companies.

The unfairness of this action toward the colored men is apparent from the fact that the Inspector General of the Army, who went to Texas upon the President's direction, reported that he could not find any evidence of an understanding between the men. The charge of "a conspiracy of silence" existed nowhere except in Theodore Roosevelt's mind. In addition to this, the white officers of the companies, who were responsible for the conduct of the men, were not even mentioned in the order.

The dismissal of these brave and innocent men under such unfair and unjust conditions created a feeling of indignation which was not confined to the Afro-American newspapers or citizenship. President Roosevelt was condemned in all directions. Republican and Democratic newspapers forgot party lines in a common appeal for justice, while Roosevelt's name was held up to scorn in mass meetings throughout the United States. No President had ever before been denounced in such unsparing terms by his fellow-citizens, irrespective of color or political affiliation. The record shows that this condemnation was richly deserved. It demonstrates that the colored man in this country cannot expect a square deal from Theodore Roosevelt.

The President's unprecedented and arbitrary action provoked criticisms even from the newspapers of the military service. The Army and Navy Journal, a conservative publication, said that it "savors of oriental methods" and that it "went beyond the power even of the Commander-in-Chief."

Theodore Roosevelt went out of his way to inflict unmerited disgrace upon the colored soldiers. In order to impose punishment for an offense of which no one had been convicted, he had to issue an executive order which was illegal, unconstitutional and unjust. It was worse than this, because it deliberately sacrificed the colored soldier to Roosevelt's inordinate ambition. It was asserted later, and never denied, that Mr. Roosevelt, knowing that no Republican had car-

ried a Southern State since reconstruction days, was ambitious to be the first Republican to break the Solid South. He was willing, therefore, to condemn the colored soldiers without a hearing in the hope of gaining more popularity in the Southern section. As a matter of fact, the only newspapers which praised him were published in the South.

With great adroitness, however, the order dismissing the colored soldiers was not dated until after the election in New York in November, 1906, so that the colored people in that State cast their vote for Hughes and in support of the administration, utterly unconscious of the blow which was in store for their people. Thousands of them said after the appearance of the order that its issuance before the election would have lost the vote of every colored man. Are these things to be forgotten, now that Theodore Roosevelt is appealing for the votes of the colored man to gratify his latest and most dangerous ambition?

Public indignation over Roosevelt's action was so great that the United States Senate ordered an investigation through its Committee on Military Affairs. Through the support of five Democrats every one from a Southern State and, therefore, prejudiced against colored soldiers and colored people, the committee was able to bring in a majority report which, in a way, sustained the President. Four Republican Senators, on the other hand, manifested a degree of fairness which was totally lacking on the part of Mr. Roosevelt. They signed their names to a report which concluded as follows:

"Therefore, having carefully considered all the testimony, we have reached the following conclusions:

"1. The testimony wholly fails to identify the particular individuals, or any of them, who participated in the shooting affray that occurred at Brownsville, Tex., on the night of August 13-14, 1906.

"2. The testimony wholly fails to show that the discharged soldiers of the Twenty-fifth U. S. Infantry, or any of them, entered into any agreement or so-called 'conspiracy of silence,' or that they had among themselves any understanding of any nature to withold any information of which they, or any or them, might be possessed concerning the shooting affray that occurred at Brownsville, Tex., on the night of August 13-14, 1906.

"3. The testimony is no contradictory, and much of it so unreliable, that it is not sufficient to sustain the charge that the soldiers of the Twenty-fifth U. S. Infantry, or any of them, participated in the shooting affray that occurred at Brownsville, Tex., on the night of August 13-14, 1906.

"4. Whereas the testimony shows that the discharged men had a good record as soldiers, and that many of them had by their long and faithful service acquired valuable rights of which they are deprived by a discharge without honor; and

"Whereas the testimony shows beyond a reasonable doubt that whatever may be the fact as to who did the shooting, many of the men so discharged were innocent of any offense in connection therewith; therefore it is, in our opinion, the duty of Congress to provide by appropriate legislation for the correction of their record and for their re-enlistment and reinstatement in the Army, and for the restoration to them of all the rights of which they have been deprived, and we so recommend.

N. B. SCOTT.
J. B. FORAKER.
J. A. HEMENWAY.
M. G. BULKELEY.

Roosevelt's injudicious handling of the Brownsville affair was a discredit to his record as President. As this broadside, published anonymously, underscores, Roosevelt was criticized by the northern and black press, and by several dissenters of a Senate committee, which upheld the President's decision after a special hearing. Yet no soldier was ever tried for a criminal offense, and fourteen soldiers were later found to be eligible for reenlistment. In 1972, the United States Army reversed all of the dishonorable discharges to honorable.

"Roosevelt's Hostility to the Colored People of the United States—The Record of the Discharge of the Colored Soldiers at Brownsville," broadside, 1907. RARE BOOKS DIVISION, LIBRARY OF CONGRESS, WASHINGTON, D.C.

It was Roosevelt's good fortune as President (1901–1909) to have served during times of peace and prosperity. In this cartoon by Edward Kemble, Roosevelt serves the "Prosperity" bird to Uncle Sam, while such Roosevelt initiatives as the "Pure Food Bill" and "Meat Inspection" fill the table.

Uncle Sam: "For the Chef, the bird, and the little side issues let us be truly thankful. For these mercies are we truly thankful." by Edward W. Kemble (1861–1933), pen and ink, 33.7 x 29.2 cm. (13¼ x 11½ in.), for *Collier's*, December 1, 1906. THEODORE ROOSEVELT BIRTHPLACE NATIONAL HISTORIC SITE, NATIONAL PARK SERVICE, NEW YORK CITY

PUCK

"HOW THE DIABOLO CAN I KEEP THIS GOING TILL —"

In this cartoon of President Roosevelt attempting to sustain William H. Taft's nomination for the presidency, the artist plays upon Taft's excessive weight of more than 350 pounds.

How the Diablo Can I Keep This Going Till Nomination Day? by Udo J. Keppler (1872–1956), hand-colored lithographic proof, 51.4 x 36.2 cm. (20¼ x 14 ¼ in.), for *Puck,* December 11, 1907. Theodore Roosevelt Birthplace National Historic Site, National Park Service, New York City

Supreme Court Justice David J. Brewer used to jest that William Howard Taft (1857–1930) was the politest man in Washington; he was perfectly capable of giving up his seat on a streetcar to three ladies. Taft's amicable disposition—it was said that his laugh was one of the "great American institutions"—was the foremost quality that won Roosevelt's admiration. As governor general of the Philippines and then as secretary of war, Taft proved to be a troubleshooter in Roosevelt's cabinet. His longtime ambition had been to someday sit with Justice Brewer on the bench of the Supreme Court. Taft would ultimately succeed to the Court, but not before Roosevelt pegged him to be his successor. "Taft will carry on the work substantially as I have carried it on," predicted Roosevelt. "His policies, principles, purposes and ideals are the same as mine." Yet when Taft later proved to be his own person, Roosevelt was distraught. Taft failed to convey the spirit of progressivism to which Roosevelt was ever leaning.

William Howard Taft by William Valentine Schevill (1864–1951), oil on artist board, 85.1 x 74.9 cm. (33½ x 29½ in.), circa 1908–1912. National Portrait Gallery, Smithsonian Institution, Washington, D.C.; gift of William E. Schevill

Canal construction began in 1904 and was not completed until 1914. In a cartoon for the *New York Herald* titled *The News Reaches Bogotá,* William A. Rogers depicted a giant-sized Roosevelt in Panama throwing a spadeful of dirt on Bogotá, the Colombian capital. Roosevelt's zealous diplomacy hurt his reputation and left many Latin American countries wary of future American intentions. Contributing to their unease was Roosevelt's corollary to the Monroe Doctrine, which now committed American intervention, if necessary, to maintain peace in the Western Hemisphere.

Yet in fairness to Roosevelt's foreign policy, it was more than just Big Stick diplomacy. The President proved himself to be a skillful international arbiter. In 1903 he successfully mediated an Alaskan boundary dispute with Canada and Great Britain, and in 1906 he intervened to prevent Germany and France from resorting to hostilities over the dominion of Morocco. The Treaty of Portsmouth of 1905, ending the Russo-Japanese War, was Roosevelt's proudest diplomatic moment. For bringing the two sides successfully together at the peace table in Portsmouth, New Hampshire, Roosevelt won the Nobel Peace Prize in 1906. Although the administration had viewed the Russians as being the most potentially threatening of the two, in the end the Japanese grumbled the most about the peace. Relations with Japan deteriorated as the United States sought to limit Japanese immigration, while protecting the Open Door policy in Asia. In a gesture of American might and will, Roosevelt ordered a fleet of newly painted battleships, the Great White Fleet, on a fourteen-month tour around the world. Arriving back home only days before the President left office, the expedition demonstrated the administration's foreign policy of peace through strength.

TR's energetic leadership made Americans feel good about themselves and their country. In 1904 they elected Roosevelt by the largest popular majority to that time over the Democratic challenger, Judge Alton Parker of New York. Not wishing to break precedent and serve more than eight years, Roosevelt announced that he would not seek reelection. His wife Edith was stunned. She knew that he would regret it, and

"To my mind, this building of the canal through Panama will rank in kind, though not of course in degree, with the Louisiana Purchase and the acquisition of Texas."

he sorely did, although he never admitted as much. In effect, he made himself a lame-duck President, especially in his last two years in office. Moreover, Roosevelt's politics had become more progressive, steadily moving him away from the center. Conservatives in Congress were firmly in control, thereby thwarting much of his power. Still, he maintained his popularity with the people and his control of the Republican Party. Like Andrew Jackson had done seventy-two years before, Roosevelt handpicked his successor, Secretary of War William Howard Taft. Taft had wide experience in foreign affairs and was a loyal progressive. Roosevelt thought he would be the best candidate to continue his reform policies. He was also amiable and easygoing, and handily defeated the Democratic challenger, William Jennings Bryan, in the election of 1908. For Roosevelt, the biggest challenge of his life now was to keep himself relevant in a world in which he no longer played a leading part. He would ponder his options during the next year, while on a safari in Africa.

1. Morris, *Roosevelt*, p. 740; Roosevelt to Lodge, September 23, 1901, *Letters*, vol. 3, p. 150.

2. Morris, *Roosevelt*, pp. 12, 17; Roosevelt, *Autobiography*, p. 372.

3. Miller, *Roosevelt*, p. 369.

4. Pringle, *Roosevelt*, p. 4.

5. Miller, *Roosevelt*, pp. 431–34.

6. *TR Cyclopedia*, p. 327.

7. Ibid., p. 404.

8. Ibid., p. 409.

Captions:
Page 50: "Don't I!" in Charles Merrill Mount, *John Singer Sargent: A Biography* (New York, 1955), p. 246. *Page 55*: "It's just a head," in Tara Leigh Tappert, *Cecilia Beaux and the Art of Portraiture* (Washington, D.C., 1995), p. 84. *Page 60*: "By George, that *is* good!" in James Earle Fraser, "Sculpting T.R.," *American Heritage* 23 (April 1972): 97. *Page 63*: "He is an artist," Edward S. Curtis, *The North American Indian*, vol. 1 (Cambridge, Mass., 1907), p. xi. *Page 76*: "Taft will carry on," *TR Cyclopedia*, p. 595.

Chapter 3

The Restless Hunter

ONLY ONCE IN AMERICAN HISTORY had a President vacated the White House and then returned to it again as President. This had been Grover Cleveland's unique destiny in 1893. That this had occurred within recent memory, and to a politician in whose footsteps Roosevelt had followed as governor of New York and finally as President, must have given TR reason to pause as he himself became a private citizen again. He was only fifty years old, the youngest man to leave office. Cleveland had been just eighteen months older when he temporarily yielded power to Benjamin Harrison in 1889. For the record, Roosevelt claimed that he was through with politics. This was the only thing he could have said as Taft, his successor, waited in the wings. An inauguration day photograph of the two leaders on the White House portico gives the appearance of perfect accord and suggests a smooth transition of party power.

Dressed in the fashionable knee-length coats of the day, they look confidently into the camera, their hulking figures filling up the lens. The view offers no hint of the blizzard-like conditions, which had canceled the outdoor inaugural ceremony planned for the East Front of the Capitol. Perhaps this was an omen of how relations between these two national titans would soon develop. TR had enjoyed being President as much as any person possibly could. Filling the post–White House vacuum would require something big and grand, and

Before retiring as President, Roosevelt reflected on his tenure in the White House: "I have thoroughly enjoyed the job. I never felt more vigorous, so far as the work of the office is concerned. . . . However, for the very reason that I believe in being a strong President and making the most of the office and using it without regard to the little, feeble, snarling men who yell about executive usurpation, I also believe that it is not a good thing that any one man should hold it too long."

I've Had a Perfectly Corking Time (detail) by Udo J. Keppler (1872–1956), chromo-lithograph, 35.6 x 25.4 cm. (14 x 10 in.), cover for *Puck*, July 15, 1908. THEODORE ROOSEVELT INAUGURAL SITE FOUNDATION, BUFFALO, NEW YORK

with that in mind, Roosevelt planned his immediate future. The prospect of a yearlong safari in Africa brightened for him what otherwise would have been the dreary prospect of retirement. It "will let me down to private life without that dull thud of which we hear so much," he wrote.[1]

Since the days of his youth, Roosevelt had been an avid naturalist and hunter. In part, the former gave the latter a degree of legitimacy when the killing of wild animals was not for the sake of providing food. Hunting was the perfect amalgamation of Roosevelt's intellectual and physical energies. Still, trophy hunting had its own rewards. "It doesn't seem to me that there can be a much happier life than the one spent going through the waste places, in all parts of the world, after big game," Roosevelt wrote in 1898. As President, he hunted, but only sparingly, so as not to arouse undue public attention to this form of recreation. Nevertheless, a hunting trip Roosevelt made into the swamps of Mississippi in 1902 became legendary when he refused to shoot an exhausted black bear, which had been run down by a pack of hounds and roped to a tree. Although the incident was reported in the local press, Clifford K. Berryman, a staff artist for the *Washington Post,* made it memorable with a small front-page cartoon titled *Drawing the Line in Mississippi.* Roosevelt is shown holding a rifle, but refusing to shoot the bedraggled bear. The bear, however, received no executive clemency; Roosevelt ordered someone else to put the creature out of its misery. Clifford Berryman elected to keep the bear alive in his cartoons, and it evolved, ever more cuddly, as a companion to Roosevelt, ultimately spawning the Teddy Bear craze.

Prone to this kind of publicity, it was understandable why Roosevelt insisted that the press not follow him into the wilds of Africa. He was now a private citizen, he protested, and he had a right to his privacy. Still, he was no ordinary citizen, as his safari plans would have suggested, had they been generally known. He was preparing for an expedition of twelve months' duration, which he began organizing a full year before his term as President was to expire. He invited his son, Kermit, along for companionship, if the lad would be willing

Theodore Roosevelt and William H. Taft (detail) at the White House, prior to the start of inauguration ceremonies at the Capitol, March 4, 1909. THEODORE ROOSEVELT COLLECTION, HARVARD COLLEGE LIBRARY, CAMBRIDGE, MASSACHUSETTS

Clifford K. Berryman's popular little bear, which evolved into Theodore Roosevelt's sidekick in dozens of the artist's subsequent cartoons, first appeared innocuously in this illustration titled *Drawing the Line in Mississippi* (detail), in the *Washington Post*, November 16, 1902. Library of Congress, Washington, D.C.

I've Had a Perfectly Corking Time by Udo J. Keppler, see page 81.

to interrupt his first year of studies at Harvard. Kermit needed no persuading and promised to redouble his academic endeavors upon his return, which he did, finishing his four-year curriculum in two and a half years. With the help of several British experts, Roosevelt oversaw every preparation: itinerary, gear and clothing, food and provisions, weapons, personnel, and expenses. On New Year's Eve he penned a few gloating lines to President-elect Taft, who was pondering over his cabinet, "*I* in a lighthearted way have spent the morning testing the rifles for my African trip. Life has compensations!"[2]

Roosevelt was genuinely interested in the African fauna and desired that his safari be as scientific as possible. He enticed the Smithsonian Institution to join the expedition by offering to contribute extensively to its fledgling collection of wildlife specimens. The basic arrangement called for TR and Kermit to hunt and shoot, while the Smithsonian scientists supervised the preservation and shipping of the kills back to the museum for research and exhibition. Approximately thirty sponsors funded the Smithsonian's expenses; Andrew Carnegie was asked to contribute $27,000 to keep the safari

As reported in the newspapers at Christmas in 1902, following Roosevelt's famous bear hunt, the White House began receiving gifts of toy bears. Although not called Teddy Bears until several years later, the stuffed-bear craze had begun. Early makers were the Ideal Toy Company and Steiff of Germany. This bear, Teddy B, was inspired by a popular series of children's books, *The Roosevelt Bears*. SAGAMORE HILL NATIONAL HISTORIC SITE, NATIONAL PARK SERVICE, OYSTER BAY, NEW YORK

☛

The popularity of Seymour Eaton's *The Roosevelt Bears: Their Travels and Adventures* is evident from this four-sided pitcher, decorated with scenes from the storybook.

"Roosevelt Bears" pitcher by Buffalo Pottery, ceramic, 20 cm. (7⅞ in.) height, 1907. SAGAMORE HILL NATIONAL HISTORIC SITE, NATIONAL PARK SERVICE, OYSTER BAY, NEW YORK

☛

The Roosevelt Bears: Their Travels and Adventures was the first of a series of four books created between 1905 and 1907 by Paul Piper under the pen name Seymour Eaton. Arranged in verses of mirth and jingle, these fanciful stories appeared originally as serials in leading newspapers. THEODORE ROOSEVELT BIRTHPLACE NATIONAL HISTORIC SITE, NATIONAL PARK SERVICE, NEW YORK CITY

going until its scheduled end. To cover personal expenses for Kermit and himself, which ran to about $20,000, TR signed a $50,000 contract with *Scribner's* to write a series of articles to be compiled in a book.

On March 23, three weeks after the inauguration, the Roosevelts sailed out of New York harbor aboard the steamer *Hamburg,* amid cheers from well-wishers and dignitaries. TR took with him some two hundred large cases containing the civilized comforts that would see him through his African experience. A particularly indispensable item was a case of some sixty volumes of literature he had chosen, which had been individually bound in pigskin, a gift from his sister Corinne. The special leather coverings would protect the books from the "blood, sweat, gun-oil, dust, and ashes" with which they would inevitably come in contact. His inventory included the Bible and dozens of classics by Dickens, Thackeray, Goethe, Shakespeare, and others, in addition to Homer in Greek and Dante in Italian.[3] With one of three hunting rifles in hand and a copy of *Alice in Wonderland,* or perhaps *The Federalist,* in his pocket, Roosevelt would become the most exotic creature in all of Africa.

On the day the Roosevelts set sail, the *New York Evening Mail* recorded the event with a cartoon by Homer Davenport. He depicted several species of African wildlife—a lion, an elephant, a giraffe, a zebra, a hyena, among others—all taking refuge in the top of a tree, and scanning the horizon for danger. A monkey on the ground carries a ladder and runs to join them. The caption, "Hist! See who's coming!" needed no further explanation. Davenport's cartoon derived its humor by taking the animals' point of view, an approach adopted by fellow artists in dozens of later cartoons. Not surprisingly, Roosevelt's adversaries in Congress and certain industrialists expressed similar sympathies for the welfare of the African fauna. J. Pierpont Morgan allegedly said that he hoped the first lion TR encountered would do its duty.

Roosevelt detested long ocean voyages. The trip to British East Africa, via Gibraltar and Naples, where the party transferred to another ship, and then to Messina, took nearly a full month. On April 21, the Roosevelt party landed at Mombasa, in

Kermit and Theodore Roosevelt (detail) with the first of ten Cape buffalo they would shoot during their African safari, by an unidentified photographer, photograph, 10.5 x 8.2 cm. (4⅛ x 3¼ in.), circa 1909. EDMUND HELLER PAPERS, SMITHSONIAN INSTITUTION ARCHIVES, WASHINGTON, D.C.

☛

Roosevelt made extensive scientific notes about his African expedition. His interests far exceeded the rudiments of stalking and shooting big game. For instance, he was keenly interested in the flora of Africa, and recorded the dietary habits of the animals he killed after examining the contents of their stomachs.

The First Bull Elephant (detail) by R. J. Cuninghame (lifedates unknown), photograph, 8.9 x 14.6 cm. (3½ x 5¾ in.), 1909. Published in Roosevelt's *African Game Trails.* EDMUND HELLER PAPERS, SMITHSONIAN INSTITUTION ARCHIVES, WASHINGTON, D.C.

"Last night a hippo came almost into camp; lions were roaring and elephants trumpeting within a mile; and yesterday I shot two white rhinoceroses."

present-day Kenya. The country was an unspoiled frontier of plains, deserts, and high plateaus, which supported more animal species than TR had ever before encountered. A ribbon of railroad track ran northwest through this vast wilderness to the capital city of Nairobi, 250 miles from the coast. Fourteen years of British colonization had transformed Nairobi into an outpost of taste and refinement, where tea and locally grown coffee were sipped in bone china cups, where lawn tennis was played, and where horse racing attracted natives of different tribes, notably the Swahili, the Wakamba, and the Masai, all in their traditional costumes.

The safari, one of the largest ever fielded in Africa, began on the Kapiti Plains, southeast of the capital. Roosevelt, whose meticulous preparations included studying a model of an elephant's cranium, showing the precise location of the brain, was himself impressed when it all came together, as if "some small military expedition was about to start."[4] It required 260 porters, 200 of whom were needed to carry the scientific

To commemorate the African safari, Lenox of New York produced this Toby pitcher of Roosevelt holding a rifle in one hand and a book in the other. The handle is designed in the shape of an elephant's head and trunk.

Toby pitcher designed by Edward Penfield for Lenox, ceramic, 19 cm. (7½ in.) height, 1909. THEODORE ROOSEVELT BIRTHPLACE NATIONAL HISTORIC SITE, NATIONAL PARK SERVICE, NEW YORK CITY

The Question—"Can a Champion Come Back?" by Eugene Zimmerman (1862–1935), chromolithograph, 35.6 x 25.4 cm. (14 x 10 in.), cover for *Judge,* August 6, 1910. THEODORE ROOSEVELT INAUGURAL SITE FOUNDATION, BUFFALO, NEW YORK

My Boy! was one of the numerous graphic commentaries of Roosevelt's welcome home from his African and European sojourns.

    My Boy! by Edward W. Kemble (1861–1933), chromolithograph, 40.6 x 28.3 cm. (16 x 11⅛ in.), cover for *Harper's Weekly,* June 18, 1910. LYNDON BAINES JOHNSON LIBRARY AND MUSEUM, AUSTIN, TEXAS

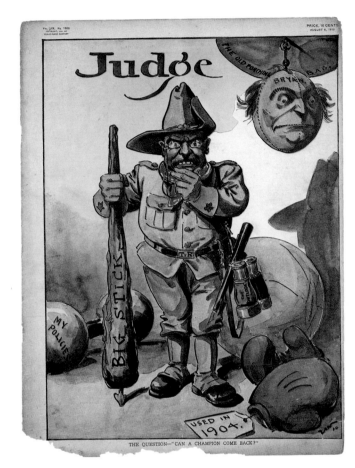

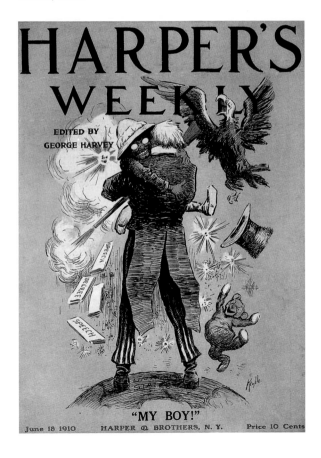

equipment of the Smithsonian's three naturalists, including four tons of salt for the curing of skins. An extremely large American flag furled over the heads of those in the front of the long human caravan, instilling Roosevelt's personal pilgrimage with a measure of national pride.

As a hunter, Roosevelt was average at best. His enthusiasm for the chase is what is remembered most, especially in his writings. Kermit, aware of his father's poor eyesight, was amazed at how deadly he could be with a gun.

The secret, said Roosevelt, was to shoot often. Moreover, the game in Africa were generally large, and unpredictably close at range. During an elephant hunt on Mount Kenya, TR barely escaped an angry bull, which rushed out of some thick brush and passed so close, he wrote afterward, "that he could have touched me with his trunk." On another occasion, Kermit shot and killed a charging leopard at six yards after it had mauled a porter.

Adventure awaited the Roosevelts at every stage of their safari as it progressed northwest across the inland sea that is Lake Victoria, through present-day Uganda, and into the Belgian Congo. From neighboring Lake Albert they reached the headwaters of the White Nile, which carried them into the Sudan. "It is the heart of the African wilderness," TR wrote to Henry Cabot Lodge in January. "Last night a hippo came almost into camp; lions were roaring and elephants trumpeting within a mile; and yesterday I shot two white rhinoceroses." Disease proved to be the most immediate and prevalent danger. A gun bearer died of fever and four porters died of dysentery. And in a nearby village eight natives died of sleeping sickness. The Roosevelts continued "in the best of health," and between father and son, they kept the Smithsonian scientists and taxidermists busy for most of the twelve months. Together they accumulated a grand total of 512 trophies, representing 79 species. TR himself recorded shooting 296 animals and birds, including 7 giraffes, 7 hippopotamuses, 8 elephants, 9 lions, 13 rhinoceroses, and 15 zebras. Later, and to his distress, he learned that the Smithsonian had room to display only 50 specimens.[5]

In the middle of March 1910, the Roosevelt-Smithsonian

*"I am received
everywhere here with
as much wild
enthusiasm as if I were
on a Presidential tour
at home."*

expedition disbanded in Khartoum, the capital of Anglo-Egyptian Sudan. TR was reunited with his wife Edith and his daughter Ethel, and together they traveled down the Nile to Cairo. Their destination was Europe. Theodore had promised Edith a long-deserved vacation. But when their plans became known, the invitations began arriving. Roosevelt was invited to give a lecture at the Sorbonne in Paris, and to give the annual Romanes Lecture at Oxford University in England. In Norway, he arranged finally to deliver his formal acceptance speech for having won the Nobel Peace Prize four years earlier. What Edith had hoped would be a quiet, private sojourn turned into a well-publicized triumphal tour for her husband, as he accepted invitations from the sovereigns of Italy, Austria-Hungary, Belgium, Holland, Germany, and Great Britain. From Copenhagen he wrote, "I am received everywhere here with as much wild enthusiasm as if I were on a Presidential tour at home." A few days later in Christiania, he gave a sitting to the Norwegian sculptor Gustav Vigeland. The Roosevelt Monument Association of North Dakota had commissioned him to design and cast a bronze equestrian statue of TR, now located on the campus of the agricultural college at Fargo.[6]

Roosevelt's presence was still being felt back home in America. When he returned to New York in June, the city staged an unprecedented reception. The ceremonies included a United States Navy escort into the harbor, two twenty-one-gun salutes, military bands playing the "Star-Spangled Banner," an official welcoming party of two hundred greeters, a reunion of Rough Riders, and a parade, whose route was lined with Roosevelt's proud former police force, managing a crowd estimated at a million people. Newspapers and journals took up the applause. *Harper's*, *Puck*, and *Collier's*, to name just three, ran illustrated caricatures of Roosevelt on their covers. Reporters pressed TR for his views on the state of the country in the hands of President Taft. For the time being, he could not be coaxed into speaking publicly. Yet there remained an air of expectation.

Privately, Roosevelt had grave misgivings about his successor. Letters of alarm about Taft's dalliances with the Old Guard faction of the Republican Party had reached him in

Africa. Passage of the excessively protectionist Payne-Aldrich Tariff and Taft's dismissal of Gifford Pinchot, chief of the United States Forest Service, deepened the chasm within the party between conservatives and progressives, and sent alarmists complaining to Roosevelt about the President's new-found conservatism, his nod to big business, and his ambivalence about conservation measures. In reality, Taft's administration was not entirely a reversal of Roosevelt's; Taft, for instance, initiated more antitrust suits than the trust-buster had done himself. Although Taft's record on conservation was poor, and he did not press to expand TR's reforms in labor and regulatory legislation, Taft's alleged sins were in large part matters of presidential style. The President, said Roosevelt privately at first, was too much of a follower. "He is evidently a man who takes color from his surroundings. He was an excellent man under me."[7]

Roosevelt simply could not restrain either his ego or his love of politics. Coaxed by his admirers, he was back in the fray by the end of summer. In August he successfully challenged the leadership of the state party machine in New York, before embarking on a sixteen-state lecture tour espousing the tenets of his "New Nationalism." Roosevelt was calling for the government to play a more active role to promote the welfare of its citizens. In a speech he delivered on August 31 in Osawatomie, Kansas, he called for graduated income and inheritance taxes, health insurance, and direct primaries for state delegates chosen to the national conventions. These were radical proposals by any standard of the day. Many considered them to be socialistic. The more Roosevelt talked, the more he sounded as if he were running for President again. Eugene Zimmerman's cover illustration for *Judge* on August 6, 1910, posed the question, "Can a champion come back?" Zimmerman portrayed a quizzical-looking TR dressed in his colonel's uniform, clutching a Big Stick in one hand and rubbing his chin with the other. A variety of sporting implements surround him, including a barbell labeled "My Policies," a pair of boxing gloves labeled "Used in 1904," and a punching bag bearing the likeness of William Jennings Bryan, the Democratic Party's unsuccessful presidential candidate in

The President, said Roosevelt privately at first, was too much of a follower. "He is evidently a man who takes color from his surroundings. He was an excellent man under me."

Oscar E. Cesare's cartoon, *Bully for Illinois! Delighted!* appeared in the *New York Sun* on April 11, 1912, and referred to Roosevelt's success in winning the Illinois Republican presidential primary. When Roosevelt won the Pennsylvania primary four days later, it sent a message to President Taft that his renomination would not necessarily be a certainty. For the first time in history, an incumbent President had to actively campaign for his party's renomination.

Bully for Illinois! Delighted! by Oscar E. Cesare (1885–1948), charcoal with opaque white on paper, 33 x 29.2 cm. (13 x 11½ in.), for the *New York Sun*, April 11, 1912. Theodore Roosevelt Collection, Harvard College Library, Cambridge, Massachusetts. By permission of the Houghton Library, Harvard University

three of the last four elections. A fountain pen hangs at TR's side in place of a sword, along with a pair of binoculars labeled "The Outlook." Before leaving the White House, Roosevelt had agreed to be a contributing editor for the *Outlook,* a weekly journal of public opinion closely aligned with Roosevelt's own views.

TR's bid for a third presidential term began in earnest in late February 1912, when he announced that he would accept the GOP nomination if it were tendered to him. This was a monumental decision on his part, one he made contrary to his own established belief in the tradition of party loyalty. He declared himself without the full backing of party leaders, not even that of his good friend Senator Lodge. Roosevelt was counting on winning the support of the people, and was successful in those states that had direct primaries. But in June, at the Republican convention in Chicago, the party machine wrested control of the proceedings and nominated Taft easily after the Roosevelt delegates had walked out. This was the

THE LATEST ARRIVAL AT THE POLITICAL ZOO

DRAWN BY E. W. KEMBLE

The Latest Arrival at the Political Zoo by Edward W. Kemble (1861–1933), lithograph, 34.3 x 23.8 cm. (13½ x 9⅜ in.), for *Harper's Weekly,* July 20, 1912. THEODORE ROOSEVELT BIRTHPLACE NATIONAL HISTORIC SITE, NATIONAL PARK SERVICE, NEW YORK CITY

start of the Progressive Party, from which Roosevelt gratefully accepted the nomination. Ultimately, as he had feared in private, this political foray would be akin to charging up San Juan Hill unarmed. TR's candidacy generated enthusiasm in what would become a historic election. The press was especially happy to have him back in the running. From the moment he declared, "My hat is in the ring," he became the most visible, if not viable, candidate.[8] A. W. Brewerton, a cartoonist for the *Atlanta Journal,* spoke for his colleagues in a cartoon titled

On October 14, 1912, Roosevelt was leaving a hotel in Milwaukee when he was shot in the chest by a crazed man, who denounced the candidate's unprecedented bid for a third presidential term. The bullet passed through Roosevelt's eyeglass case and the reading copy of a campaign speech he was preparing to give. Roosevelt, holding a handkerchief to his bleeding chest, refused immediate medical assistance and proceeded to give his nearly one-hour-long speech as planned. Holding the bullet-pierced speech up to the crowd, Roosevelt said, "You see it takes more than that to kill a bull moose." Only afterward did he consent to enter a hospital to have his wound thoroughly examined.

Page one of a telegram announcing that President Roosevelt had been shot, but not seriously wounded. THEODORE ROOSEVELT INAUGURAL SITE FOUNDATION, BUFFALO, NEW YORK

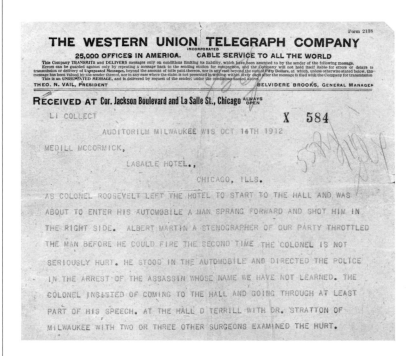

Where Teddy's Announcement Caused Joy. He depicted an artist's studio filled with pictures of TR, and two cartoonists embracing joyfully upon learning of Roosevelt's decision. "How could we do without him?" one says to the other.

From every angle, the cartoonists exploited Roosevelt's platform, which called for government regulation of major corporations, women's suffrage, and social justice reforms on behalf of labor and the poor. Using pen and ink they countered TR's idealism with adroit satire. In one of the most memorable cartoons of the campaign, titled *The Latest Arrival at the Political Zoo,* Edward W. Kemble caricatured the heart and soul of the Progressive Party itself. TR is portrayed as the party mascot, a bespectacled and grinning bull moose. In the background a bandaged elephant says to a donkey, emblems of the two major parties, "Suffering snakes. How Theodore has changed." In this and in hundreds of other cartoons, the image of Roosevelt would dominate the campaign. It was almost as if he were the only candidate. Yet in the end, it was Woodrow Wilson's progressive platform—the New Freedom, which

This TR bandanna was made into a hat during the Bull Moose campaign of 1912. THEODORE ROOSEVELT BIRTHPLACE NATIONAL HISTORIC SITE, NATIONAL PARK SERVICE, NEW YORK CITY

In 1916, Oscar Cesare caricatured the end of the Bull Moose party after Roosevelt refused to run for President as the Progressive candidate.
Alas Poor Yorick! by Oscar E. Cesare (1885–1948), india ink over pencil on paper, 47.4 x 32.5 cm. (18¹¹/₁₆ x 12¾ in.), for the *New York Sun*, April 8, 1916. NATIONAL PORTRAIT GALLERY, SMITHSONIAN INSTITUTION, WASHINGTON, D.C.; GIFT OF MR. VALENTINE CESARE

called for less government intervention than what Roosevelt was proposing—that won the election for the Democratic Party. Roosevelt finished a respectable second, beating Taft soundly by eighty electoral votes.

If the result was not what TR had wanted, it was what he had expected. The election confirmed the entrenchment of the two-party system in American politics, and not even a candidate as popular as Theodore Roosevelt could influence enough of the people to break with tradition. Although the Progressive Party nominated Roosevelt again in 1916, he refused to accept. He realized that the Bull Moose party had been crushed in the last election and that, practically speaking, it was a one-man party with no future. Had Roosevelt remained loyal to Taft in 1912, the Republicans might well have nominated him four years later. Under the circumstances, he was passed over for another former New York governor, Supreme Court Justice Charles Evans Hughes.

In the weeks and months after the election, Roosevelt began writing his autobiography. Writing, although arduous at times, had always been a relaxing exercise for him, given his frenetic energy, much as talking is for the loquacious. (He was that, too.) The opportunity to tell his own story came at a welcome time in his life, one in which there were days to fill and no better topics to discuss. It was a chance for him to relive his youth, to rope cattle again in the West, and of course, to review his extraordinary career of public service. Published in 1913, the *Autobiography* is noteworthy for its deletions, namely any mention of his first wife, Alice Lee, and any analysis of the historic election of 1912. By ending the text abruptly with his leaving the presidency, TR could not have expressed better with words the tremendous void he felt in his life.

An invitation to visit South America in the fall of 1913, to lecture and then to embark upon a scientific jungle expedition, proved to be timely indeed. Roosevelt could not resist another adventure; it was his last chance to be a boy, he said. In February 1914, together with his son Kermit and a number of Brazilian naturalists, Roosevelt began an exploration of the Rio da Dúvida (River of Doubt), an uncharted river running north toward the equator through the interior of Brazil.

JAMES MONTGOMERY FLAGG
1 9 1 4

The drawings of James Montgomery Flagg, appearing in books and magazines, and bearing the artist's bold, full signature, were popular during the Roosevelt era. Flagg, like Roosevelt, espoused favorite American themes in much of his work, namely devotion to family and country. His World War I posters have become icons of national patriotism. In 1914, the year the war began, Flagg demonstrated his skills as a portraitist in this sensitive sketch of Roosevelt in retirement.

Theodore Roosevelt by James Montgomery Flagg (1877–1960), pencil on artist board, 33 x 32.7 cm. (13 x 12⅞ in.), 1914. THEODORE ROOSEVELT BIRTHPLACE NATIONAL HISTORIC SITE, NATIONAL PARK SERVICE, NEW YORK CITY

For Roosevelt, marching off to fight in the European war would have been another adventure in living what he once called "the strenuous life." President Wilson, although sympathetic, never seriously considered his offer to serve in the army.

Theodore Roosevelt and Woodrow Wilson by William C. Morris (1874–1940), pen and ink, 39.4 x 34 cm. (15½ x 13⅜ in.), 1916. THEODORE ROOSEVELT COLLECTION, HARVARD COLLEGE LIBRARY, CAMBRIDGE, MASSACHUSETTS. BY PERMISSION OF THE HOUGHTON LIBRARY, HARVARD UNIVERSITY

During his last years, Roosevelt continued to be a national presence. In addition to his writings, he spoke on behalf of the war effort to dozens of missionary and service organizations throughout the country. Here he is speaking to a crowd from the back of a railroad car in 1918.

Theodore Roosevelt (detail) by Edith Hughes (lifedates unknown), gelatin silver print, 20.7 x 28.8 cm. (8 ⅛ x 11⁵⁄₁₆ in.), 1918. NATIONAL PORTRAIT GALLERY, SMITHSONIAN INSTITUTION, WASHINGTON, D.C.; GIFT OF JOANNA STURM [not in exhibition]

Treacherous currents and rapids, which seemingly appeared from nowhere, frequently left the party hauling their dugout canoes through the dense jungle. For forty-eight days they did not encounter another human being. Snakes and mosquitoes were constant menaces during their nearly one-thousand-mile journey. At one point, they exhausted their supply of preserved food. One man drowned. Another was murdered. The crazed assailant fled into the jungle and presumably did not survive. Like others in the party, Roosevelt suffered from tropical fever. He wrote to his editor at *Scribner's*, for whom he was writing a series of articles, that his temperature was 105 degrees. More serious was a leg gash he suffered when a canoe smashed him against a rock. For days he could not walk, and he even suggested that he be left behind. When

Roosevelt arrived back in New York in the middle of May, he was using a cane and he had lost more than fifty pounds. In tribute to his courage, the Brazilian government renamed the River of Doubt, Rio Roosevelt.

Roosevelt was fifty-five, broken in health and susceptible to recurring bouts of fever for the rest of his life. His interest in national affairs and progressive politics had not waned, however. Nor had his pride in his former accomplishments. President Woodrow Wilson became TR's greatest vexation after he learned of the treaty negotiated with Colombia in the spring of 1914, offering an apology and an indemnity of $25 million for the secession of Panama. The start of World War I that summer offered Roosevelt an issue that caused him to cross swords with Woodrow Wilson, perhaps the only man he had ever come to despise. In May 1915, a German submarine sank the passenger liner *Lusitania,* killing more than 1,100

people, including 128 Americans. Wilson issued the Germans a sharp rebuke. Roosevelt, however, demanded action.

In the months leading up to America's entry into the war, Roosevelt became the nation's foremost advocate for preparedness in his speeches and writings. He even began laying plans to raise a division of volunteer mounted infantry. A 1916 cartoon by freelance artist William C. Morris depicted Roosevelt, in uniform and fully armed, at the President's desk offering his services. TR was granted his much-sought-after interview with Wilson on April 9, 1917, three days after Congress had declared a state of war with Germany. The Colonel's enthusiasm was as engaging as ever. "There is a sweetness about him that is very compelling," said Wilson afterwards to his secretary. "You can't resist the man."[9]

In spite of Roosevelt's repeated pleas to the secretary of war, the administration declined his offers to recruit or participate directly in the conflict. This would be a modern war, commanded and fought largely by younger, professionally trained soldiers, such as Douglas MacArthur and George C. Marshall, not to mention Roosevelt's own four sons. They would more than uphold the family honor which had been won two decades earlier on San Juan Hill. In July 1918, the youngest, Quentin, died in aerial combat over Château-Thierry in northern France, and two of his other boys suffered wounds. Frustrated by circumstances beyond his control, he wrote, "it is very bitter to me that I was not allowed to face the danger with my sons." On November 11, the day of the armistice ending the war, Roosevelt was hospitalized with inflammatory rheumatism. He was released in time to spend Christmas and New Year's Day at his home at Oyster Bay. "I wonder if you will ever know how I love Sagamore Hill," he said to his wife Edith as she rose to leave his room that last evening.[10] In the predawn hours of January 6, 1919, Theodore Roosevelt died in his sleep from an embolism.

Jay N. Darling's memorial cartoon, *The Long, Long Trail,* appeared in the *Des Moines* (Iowa) *Register* on January 7, 1919, the day after Roosevelt died. Based on a cartoon Darling had done two years earlier, when Buffalo Bill died, this image of TR riding off into eternity became instantly popular and was reprinted at the time, and later was cast into bronze relief plaques. The image reproduced here was the final proof for an engraved series.

The Long, Long Trail by Jay N. Darling (1876–1962), final lithographic proof, 29.2 x 22.9 cm. (11½ x 9 in.), 1919. THEODORE ROOSEVELT COLLECTION, HARVARD COLLEGE LIBRARY, CAMBRIDGE, MASSACHUSETTS. BY PERMISSION OF THE HOUGHTON LIBRARY, HARVARD UNIVERSITY

1. Joseph L. Gardner, *Departing Glory: Theodore Roosevelt as Ex-President* (New York, 1973), p. 110.
2. Roosevelt to Taft, December 31, 1908, *Letters,* vol. 6, p. 1454.
3. Gardner, *Departing Glory,* p. 112.
4. Ibid., p. 118.
5. Roosevelt to Lodge, January 17 and February 5, 1910, *Letters,* vol. 7, pp. 46–47; Mario R. DiNunzio, ed., *Theodore Roosevelt, an American Mind: A Selection from His Writings* (New York, 1994), p. 223; Emily Hahn, "'My dear Selous . . . ,'" *American Heritage* 14 (April 1963): 96.
6. Roosevelt to Robert Bacon, May 2, 1910, Roosevelt to Louis Benjamin Hanna, May 6, 1910, *Letters,* vol. 7, pp. 79, 82.
7. Roosevelt to Pinchot, June 28, 1910, ibid., p. 96.
8. Ibid., p. 508n.
9. Pringle, *Roosevelt,* p. 595.
10. Roosevelt to Georges Clemenceau, July 25, 1918, *Letters,* vol. 8, p. 1355; Gardner, *Departing Glory,* p. 399.

Captions
Page 80: "I have thoroughly enjoyed," *TR Cyclopedia,* p. 463. *Page 95*: "You see it takes," in Oscar K. Davis to Medill McCormick, telegram, October 14, 1912, Theodore Roosevelt Inaugural Site, Buffalo, New York.

A Constant Pleasure

Theodore Roosevelt at Sagamore Hill

Amy Verone

T HEODORE ROOSEVELT first came to Oyster Bay as a boy, to visit his grandfather Cornelius, who had built a summer home in the small fishing community. Two of Cornelius's five sons, Silas and James, had followed their father and built homes on the Cove Neck peninsula east of the village. In 1874 a third son, Theodore, and his wife Martha decided that they too should join the family in this tranquil area of Long Island. Their children were growing up—Anna, the oldest, was nineteen, Theodore Jr. would be sixteen in October, Elliott was fourteen, and Corinne was twelve. In part, so that the children could spend more time with their relatives, Theodore Sr. rented a house near his brothers and named it Tranquility.

Young Theodore, or "Thee," was especially fond of life in Oyster Bay. Awkward with outsiders, he was a center of attention at the gatherings attended by his cousins and a small circle of friends. One of his closest companions was Edith Carow, a childhood friend of Corinne's. He named his rowboat after her, but she was not the only girl he favored.

In 1876, Theodore left for Harvard. In his senior year, he became engaged to Alice Hathaway Lee, the cousin of a Harvard classmate; they decided to marry in the fall. That summer, Theodore purchased 155 acres of farmland on Cove Neck. He had convinced Alice that they should build their home in Oyster Bay. When she expressed concern about living so far out in the country, he reassured her that they would be part of a "community of Roosevelts." Theodore and Alice were married in Brookline, Massachusetts, on October 27, 1880, the groom's

After all, fond as I am of the White House and much though I have appreciated these years in it, there isn't any place in the world like home—like Sagamore Hill.

*—*THEODORE ROOSEVELT, JUNE 11, 1906[1]

Sagamore Hill, 1905. SAGAMORE HILL
NATIONAL HISTORIC SITE, NATIONAL PARK
SERVICE, OYSTER BAY, NEW YORK

twenty-second birthday. The newlyweds spent a two-week honeymoon at Tranquility, and then moved into an apartment in New York City.

By 1883, Theodore and Alice had contracted with the architectural firm Lamb & Rich to design their home. The house would be located on the summit of a hill and would overlook Oyster Bay and the Long Island Sound. The design was based on a layout that Theodore sketched out on an envelope. He wanted a house with a large piazza facing the water, a library and parlor, ten bedrooms for family and guests, and large fireplaces. The property would be called Leeholm, in honor of Alice's family, and would operate as a working farm. The income from the farm would offset the costs of maintaining the property. Lamb & Rich designed a stable and lodge complex, to be located just behind the main house and serve as headquarters for the farm operation.

By the winter of 1884, the stable complex was completed, and the farm manager, Noah Seaman, and his family had moved into the lodge. The plans had been finalized for the house, but the couple had not yet contracted with a builder. They were preoccupied—Alice was expecting their first child, and Theodore was serving his third term in the New York State Assembly. He was in Albany when Alice went into labor; she gave birth to a daughter on February 12, 1884. Theodore received the news by telegram; several hours later, he received another telegram telling him to come home at once. On February 14, 1884, at 3:00 a.m., his mother, Martha, died of typhoid. Alice died eleven hours later of Bright's disease; it was the fourth anniversary of her engagement to Theodore. Alice and Martha were buried at Greenwood Cemetery in Brooklyn, beside Theodore Sr., who had died of stomach cancer in 1878.

Stunned and uncertain about his future, Theodore decided to make a clean break with his old life. He would go to the Dakota Territory, where he and his brother Elliott had camped and hunted the previous summer, and try his hand at ranching. Unprepared to raise his daughter alone, he asked his sister Anna (called "Bamie") to care for her. Bamie agreed, but convinced him that he would need a home for little Alice. He signed a contract with John Wood to build the house in March 1884 and left for Albany to serve out his term. Bamie would oversee construction of the house in Oyster Bay and work to establish the farm operation.

Roosevelt spent the next two years shuttling back and forth between his ranch and New York. His house, now called Sagamore Hill, was completed in early 1885. An apple orchard had been planted on a hill overlooking Cold Spring Harbor. Several outbuildings—garden and toolsheds, cowsheds, and a chicken coop with a fenced yard—had been built around the farmyard behind the stable. During a visit to his new home in the fall of 1885, he hosted a meeting of the Meadowbrook Hunt Club, took part in a foxhunt, and resumed his friendship with Edith Kermit Carow. In November, he asked her to marry him, and she accepted. They agreed to wait a year and told no one about their engagement. On December 2, 1886, Theodore and Edith were married in London, and they spent the next two months on a honeymoon trip through Europe.

In late April 1887, the newlyweds moved into Sagamore Hill. Theodore's share of his parents' furniture had already been installed in the house. He claimed the library as an office; Edith took over the drawing room across the hall. She filled the room with family pieces from her Carow and Kermit ancestors. Furniture they had purchased together in Italy was moved into

Mame Ledwith driving Kermit and Ethel in the pony cart, circa 1895. THEODORE ROOSEVELT COLLECTION, HARVARD COLLEGE LIBRARY, CAMBRIDGE, MASSACHUSETTS

Theodore and the cousins playing football, circa 1896. SAGAMORE HILL NATIONAL HISTORIC SITE, NATIONAL PARK SERVICE, OYSTER BAY, NEW YORK

the dining room and a guest room upstairs.

Theodore's new family settled into a routine. He began writing a biography of Gouverneur Morris, while Edith spent her mornings organizing the household, sewing, and writing letters. They spent their afternoons together, playing with three-year-old Alice, riding, walking in the woods, swimming, and picnicking on the beach. They were especially fond of rowing on the Sound. As Theodore rowed, Edith would read aloud to him. Often they visited Theodore's Uncle James or his cousins, Emlen and West, who had built homes on properties adjoining Sagamore Hill. Among the three younger households, there would in time be sixteen Roosevelt children growing up on Cove Neck.

In September 1887, their first child, Theodore Jr., was born, delivered by Cousin West, a doctor who was roused out of bed when the baby arrived before the midwife. Mame Ledwith, who had been Edith's nurse, came to live with them. She would stay for the next twenty years, looking after each new baby. Kermit was born in 1889, followed by Ethel in 1891, Archie in 1894, and Quentin in 1897.

Theodore and Edith were delighted with their children and included them in all of their activities. Theodore would pull a wagon along and when "the very smallest pairs of feet grew tired of trudging bravely after us, or of racing on rapturous side trips after flowers and other treasures, the owners would clamber into the wagon" and ride home.[2] He purchased a cart and a pony named General Grant, so that the children could follow along when he and Edith went riding. From an early age, they ate in the dining room rather than the nursery; even when there were guests, they were encouraged to speak up and join in the adults' conversations. Theodore and Edith read to their children every day, and helped them memorize poems and hymns. As his "bunnies" grew, Theodore carried them on his shoulders, played tag and football in the front yard, and told ghost stories or engaged in pillow fights before bed. Theodore wrote that the children "were never allowed to be disobedient or to shirk lessons or work; and they were encouraged to have all the fun possible."[3]

Edith let the children go barefoot and dressed them casually so they could play without worrying if their clothes got dirty or torn. Theodore had a bathhouse and float built at the beach and taught his children and their younger cousins to swim and dive. Cousin Emlen taught the boys to fish and had his boatman keep fishing rods and fresh bait on his dock for them. Ted once carried a string of fish into the parlor to show his mother—the string broke and eighty-five small mackerel fell onto the carpet. Theodore and his cousins organized relay races and obstacle courses for their children in the hayloft of an old barn and rowing expeditions and picnics on the beaches around Cove Neck.

The children had free run of the farm. They made pets out of the livestock, naming their favorite cows, chickens, and pigs. Theodore wrote, "I doubt whether I ever saw Mame really offended with them except once when, out of pure but misunderstood affection, they named a pig after her."[4] There was an endless stream of pets, including ponies, dogs, cats, rabbits, turtles, snakes, and, briefly, a badger and a bear cub. They were particularly fond of guinea pigs and gave them dramatic names like Fighting Bob Evans and Admiral Dewey. A pet cemetery was established behind the house after Edith caught Ted and Ethel burying dead guinea pigs in their sandbox.

It was Edith who managed the family finances. She tracked the household accounts closely, put her husband on an allowance, and insisted on economies. Theodore, who never learned how to handle money, confessed to a friend, "Every morning Edie puts twenty dollars in my pocket, and to save my life I never can tell her afterward what I did with it!"[5]

Edith also kept the accounts for the farm operation and worked with Seaman to improve the property. A cornfield was planted between the house and farmyard to buffer the noises and smells; outer fields were planted with wheat, rye, and hay. There were pastures for the horses and a small dairy herd, as well as a large pigpen. Fruit trees and a three-acre garden for flowers and vegetables were planted behind the stable.

Sagamore Hill was not an easy property to run. The farm staff included the manager, gardener, and coachman, all of whom lived on the property. Local farmhands came daily to look after the livestock, do the chores and yardwork, and harvest the crops. By 1890, the household staff included a cook, waitress, nurse, maid, chambermaid, and laundress, all of whom lived in the house. As the family grew, the staff expanded to include a variety of nurses, governesses, and tutors; assorted maids and house servants; and a valet who doubled as a butler. There was only one bathroom, which was used by the children and the servants. Edith and Theodore still took their baths in a round tin bathtub that was set up in their room and then filled and emptied by hand. The house was lit with gas, which was produced in a small generating plant under the back porch. In the evenings, the family used oil lamps to read by and candles to see their way to bed.

"I doubt whether I ever saw Mame really offended with them except once when, out of pure but misunderstood affection, they named a pig after her."

Kermit, Ethel, and Ted with their guinea pigs, circa 1897. THEODORE ROOSEVELT COLLECTION, HARVARD COLLEGE LIBRARY, CAMBRIDGE, MASSACHUSETTS

Despite a coal furnace and all of Theodore's fireplaces, the house was cold and drafty in the winter.

For the first two years of his marriage, Theodore's writing allowed him to work at home, and the family was able to live at Sagamore Hill year-round. In May 1889, Theodore accepted an appointment to the United States Civil Service Commission. The family moved to Washington, D.C., but still spent their summers at Sagamore Hill.

During the summers, he led many of the children's activities. Under his charge, quiet walks were replaced by point-to-point marches that went over, under, or through, but never around, obstacles. Theodore taught the children and their cousins to play tennis on a grass court below the house and to shoot in a gully beyond the cornfield. When he thought they could be trusted with a gun, he allowed them to hunt in the woods and along the shore. Once, however, Ted and his cousins used the red bathhouse as a target. The next day, his parents decided to go swimming with several of Edith's friends. When Theodore modeled his new bathing suit, the ladies discovered that its seat had been "punctured with a series of holes like the bottom of a sieve."[6]

In the spring of 1895, Theodore was named to the New York City Police Commission, and the family moved back to Sagamore Hill. Theodore and Edith enrolled Ted and Kermit in the Cove Neck school with the children of the local baymen and farmers. That Christmas, Theodore was invited to speak at the school assembly. There, he addressed the children as "my little oysters" and urged them to stand up for themselves, be kind to animals, and to do something worthwhile when they grew up. It was a speech that he would repeat over the years at other assemblies and church festivals.[7]

In April 1897, Theodore was named assistant secretary of the navy by President William McKinley. The family moved to Washington in the fall, but came back to Oyster Bay in May 1898, after Theodore had resigned his position in order to serve in the Spanish-American War. While he went to Cuba with his Rough Riders, the family spent an anxious summer at Sagamore Hill. By August, the war was over and Theodore's troops were quarantined in Montauk, at the far eastern end of Long Island. On August 20, he received a pass to visit his family. Although there was no public announcement of Theodore's arrival, a cheering crowd of 1,500 people met his train; a committee greeted him with speeches and a bonfire. The entire village was decorated with banners and flags.[8]

Newspaper accounts of the fighting in Cuba had made Theodore Roosevelt a household name across the United States and propelled him to the New York governor's office in November 1898. Two years later, he was a candidate on the Republican national ticket. When President McKinley was reelected, Theodore became Vice President.

Over the summer of 1901, Theodore made several speaking tours and went on a hunting trip to Colorado; Edith made plans to move the family to Washington. She rented a house and chose schools for the children. Then, in September, President McKinley was shot by an assassin in Buffalo, New York. When he died on September 14, 1901, Theodore became the twenty-sixth President of the United States.

Years later, Alice would recall that the family's life at Oyster Bay "was decidedly different after Father became President. We were hardly ever alone. Droves of people came down to call, or to lunch, or to spend the night. . . . The Mayflower, Dolphin, and Sylph, three government boats, were one or another, as a rule, anchored off Sagamore. The newspapermen were camped in town."[9]

Theodore's days followed a familiar pattern. Before breakfast, he would go for a short walk or ride, or play tennis with the children. He spent each morning in the library, working with his secretary, William Loeb Jr., and other aides, writing speeches and dictating letters. A telephone was installed to keep them in touch with Washington and the world. In the afternoons, Theodore met with his aides, cabinet officers, and political allies or received visitors. The family still dined together, but were often joined by staff, visitors, or houseguests. After Theodore was reelected in 1904, Edith suggested that they put an addition on the house. In 1905, the North Room was added; Edith also had two closets converted into bathrooms at the same time.

Edith understood the importance of Theodore's work, but was determined that he get a break from his responsibilities. She and Loeb tried to arrange Theodore's schedule so that he was free by mid-afternoon to swim with the children or go rowing. She also conspired with Noah Seaman to make sure that he got enough exercise. Seaman regularly told him that the farm crew was short-handed and needed extra help. James Amos, Theodore's valet, remembered that "Mr. Roosevelt loved to put in a day's work on his place with the men—particularly at haying time. . . . [He] worked through the day, knocking off at sunset and at lunch time with the others. He joked and talked with his fellow

Theodore haying, circa 1905. THEODORE ROOSEVELT COLLECTION, HARVARD COLLEGE LIBRARY, CAMBRIDGE, MASSACHUSETTS

Home, wife, children—they are what really count in life. I have heartily enjoyed many things; the Presidency, my success as a soldier, a writer, a big game hunter and explorer; but all of them put together are not for one moment to be weighed in the balance when compared with the joy I have known with your mother and all of you; and, as a merely secondary thing, this house and the life here yield me constant pleasure.

—THEODORE ROOSEVELT TO TED JR., JANUARY 1911[16]

workers, drank from the same bucket and dipper, and always insisted on Seamans . . . putting his name on the pay-roll and paying him for a day's work."[10] It was also Theodore's responsibility to cut down unwanted trees; he kept an axe handy behind the front door. Edith would stand on the piazza and point out the trees that were blocking her view of the water; Theodore would cut them down. When Amos's wife asked if they could remove a tree in front of a window, she was stunned when "in a little while the President of the United States came over and chopped down the tree for us."[11]

Being at Sagamore Hill allowed Theodore to combine his two favorite activities—practicing politics and living the strenuous life. He often invited visitors to play tennis, take a cross-country hike, or participate in obstacle races through the old barn. When naturalist John Burroughs came to discuss conservation legislation, the President told him that "he could not talk politics then, he wanted to talk and to hunt birds." Burroughs found himself being led across the fields by the President, who was "filled with the one idea of showing to his visitors the black throated green warbler!"[12]

Theodore left the White House on March 4, 1909. Back at Sagamore Hill, he and Edith resumed their old habits—walking and riding together, rowing on the bay, reading aloud in the evenings. They found it more difficult to adjust to their emptying nest than to being private citizens. Alice had married Nick Longworth in 1906, and they were still living in Washington. Ted had married Eleanor Alexander in June 1910 and moved to California. Kermit was at college, and Archie and Quentin were in boarding school. Only Ethel was living at home full-time, and she was often visiting friends and family. In a 1910 letter to Ted, Roosevelt wrote wistfully, "This summer has marked the definite end of the old Oyster Bay life that all of you children used to lead."[13] Edith wrote to Kermit that "It is a dreadful wrench for me. . . . I look back regretfully to the days when the old hen could brood you all under her wings."[14] Their life settled into new patterns—traveling and visiting with friends and anticipating their children's visits home. In January 1911, Ted wrote to tell them that their first grandchild was expected; his daughter Grace was born in August.

In 1912, Theodore ran unsuccessfully for President on the Bull Moose ticket; after the campaign, he wrote to Ethel and told her, "I *never* want to leave Sagamore Hill again."[15] To Edith's relief, Theodore returned home and resumed his writing. He collaborated on a book on African game animals and wrote his auto-biography. In April 1913, Ethel married Dr. Richard Derby; the following spring their first child, Richard, was born. Ted and Eleanor's second child, Theodore III, was also born in 1914. Meanwhile, the restless former President was recuperating from an expedition he had taken to South America that year. The trip had been strenuous; Theodore had contracted malaria and a blood infection and lost fifty-six pounds. In June, Kermit married Belle Willard in Spain; their first child, Kermit Jr., was born in 1915. By the time Quentin left home for college that September, his parents had five grandchildren to distract and entertain them.

In 1916, Kermit and Belle joined the family for Christmas. It was the last time that the entire family would be together at Sagamore Hill. The United States entered the war against Germany the following April. By May, all of the boys were in uniform; by the end of July, they were all overseas. In November, Ethel's husband left for France, and she moved back to Sagamore Hill with her children, Richard and Edith. Theodore hung a flag with five blue stars, showing five sons in service, in the library window and felt an anxiety for his four sons and son-in-law that he had never felt for himself.

Theodore did his part for the war effort, traveling the country preaching preparedness and speaking at bond rallies. Both he and Edith wrote to the boys several times a week. Having their grandchildren at Sagamore Hill was a welcome diversion from the war. Richard Derby went hand in hand with his grandfather to breakfast every morning and was his grandmother's favorite. His sister Edith was "such a darling that I want to take her up and cuddle her all of the time."[17] When Ted's children visited, Edith and Theodore read them Beatrix Potter stories and fairy tales; Theodore would take them on walks to visit the pigpen.

In February 1918, Theodore was hospitalized for three weeks. He had never completely recovered from the infection he had caught in South America. The fever recurred, and surgery was needed to relieve several large abscesses. He soon resumed his activities, but his symptoms still lingered.

In July, they received the heartbreaking news that Quentin's plane had been shot down over France. It was three days before his death was confirmed. James Amos wrote, "I was not in Oyster Bay when the news came, but I have heard how it was received. Mr. Roosevelt, after reading the dispatch, carried the sad news to his wife. Then he put his arm around her waist and together they

The family together, Christmas 1916. THEODORE ROOSEVELT COLLECTION, HARVARD COLLEGE LIBRARY, CAMBRIDGE, MASSACHUSETTS

Theodore with grandchild Archie Jr., 1918. THEODORE ROOSEVELT COLLECTION, HARVARD COLLEGE LIBRARY, CAMBRIDGE, MASSACHUSETTS

walked in silence down the path that led into the woods. Down that path I had seen them go so many times together, just like that, his arm around her waist, attentive as a young husband. . . . Now they took their sorrow there."[18]

Theodore was in the hospital again in November. His doctors released him on December 25, so that he could be home for Christmas. Theodore spent the next few days resting. Edith hired a sleep-in nurse and asked James Amos to assist her husband. He arrived at Sagamore Hill on Sunday, January 5, 1919.

Theodore spent that day quietly in his room, correcting a magazine article and finishing an editorial. Edith stayed near him, reading, writing letters, and playing solitaire; she left only to greet several callers. Once Edith looked up and caught Theodore gazing out the window at the snow. He turned to her and said, "I wonder if you will ever know how I love Sagamore Hill." Later, she would remember that it had been "a happy and wonderful day."[19] Early the next morning, on January 6, 1919, Theodore died in his sleep; he was sixty years old.

Theodore Roosevelt was buried at Young's Cemetery, barely a mile from Sagamore Hill. Edith continued to live at Sagamore Hill and survived Theodore by almost thirty years. On September 30, 1948, Edith Carow Roosevelt died and was buried beside her husband.

1. Theodore Roosevelt to Ethel Roosevelt, June 11, 1906, in Joseph Bucklin Bishop, ed., *Theodore Roosevelt's Letters to His Children* (New York, 1919), p. 165.

2. Theodore Roosevelt, *An Autobiography* (New York, 1913), p. 337.

3. Ibid., p. 341.

4. Ibid., p. 342.

5. Sylvia Jukes Morris, *Edith Kermit Roosevelt: Portrait of a First Lady* (New York, 1980), p. 139.

6. Theodore Roosevelt Jr., *All in the Family* (New York, 1929), p. 99.

7. Morris, *Edith Kermit Roosevelt*, p. 164.

8. Herman Hagedorn, *The Roosevelt Family of Sagamore Hill* (New York, 1954), p. 57.

9. Alice Roosevelt Longworth, *Crowded Hours* (New York, 1933), pp. 53–54.

10. James Amos, *Theodore Roosevelt: Hero to His Valet* (New York, 1927), pp. 84–85.

11. Ibid., p. 84.

12. John Burroughs, *Camping & Tramping with Roosevelt* (Boston, 1907), pp. 81, 82, 86.

13. Hagedorn, *Sagamore Hill*, p. 293.

14. Morris, *Edith Kermit Roosevelt*, p. 367.

15. Hagedorn, *Sagamore Hill*, p. 351.

16. Ibid., p. 297.

17. Ibid., p. 383.

18. Amos, *Hero to His Valet*, pp. 84–85.

19. Morris, *Edith Kermit Roosevelt*, p. 433.

For Further Reading

Brands, H.W. *T.R.: The Last Romantic.* New York: Basic Books, 1997.

Cutright, Paul Russell. *Theodore Roosevelt: The Making of a Conservationist.* Urbana and Chicago: University of Illinois Press, 1985.

DiNunzio, Mario R., ed. *Theodore Roosevelt: An American Mind.* New York: St. Martin's Press, 1994.

Gable, John Allen. *The Bull Moose Years: Theodore Roosevelt and the Progressive Party.* Port Washington, N.Y.: Kennikat Press Corp., 1978.

Gardner, Joseph L. *Departing Glory: Theodore Roosevelt as Ex-President.* New York: Charles Scribner's Sons, 1973.

Hagedorn, Hermann. *The Roosevelt Family of Sagamore Hill.* New York: The Macmillan Company, 1954.

Harbaugh, William Henry. *Power and Responsibility: The Life and Times of Theodore Roosevelt.* New York: Farrar, Straus and Cudahy, 1961.

Hart, Albert Bushnell, and Herbert Ronald Ferleger, eds. *Theodore Roosevelt Cyclopedia.* Oyster Bay, N.Y., and Westport, Conn.: Theodore Roosevelt Association and Meckler Corporation, 1989.

Jeffers, H. Paul. *Commissioner Roosevelt: The Story of Theodore Roosevelt and the New York City Police, 1895–1897.* New York: John Wiley & Sons, Inc., 1994.

—. *Theodore Roosevelt Goes to War, 1897–1898.* New York: John Wiley & Sons, Inc., 1996.

Lorant, Stefan. *The Life and Times of Theodore Roosevelt.* New York: Doubleday & Company, Inc., 1959.

McCullough, David. *Mornings on Horseback.* New York: Simon and Schuster, 1981.

Miller, Nathan. *Theodore Roosevelt: A Life.* New York: William Morrow and Company, Inc., 1992.

Morison, Elting E., et al., eds. *The Letters of Theodore Roosevelt.* 8 vols. Cambridge: Harvard University Press, 1951–1954.

Morris, Edmund. *The Rise of Theodore Roosevelt.* New York: Coward, McCann & Geoghegan, Inc., 1979.

Morris, Sylvia Jukes. *Edith Kermit Roosevelt: Portrait of a First Lady.* New York: Coward, McCann & Geoghegan, Inc., 1980.

Pringle, Henry F. *Theodore Roosevelt: A Biography.* New York: Harcourt, Brace and Company, 1931.

Roosevelt, Theodore. *An Autobiography.* New York: Charles Scribner's Sons, 1913.

Shaw, Albert. *A Cartoon History of Roosevelt's Career.* New York: The Review of Reviews Company, 1910.

Wagenknecht, Edward. *The Seven Worlds of Theodore Roosevelt.* New York: Longmans, Green & Co., 1958.

Photography credits

Wayne Geist: pages 9, 10, 21, 22, 23 (*Bravo!*), 28 (brand), 33 (both illustrations), 38, 40, 41, 44, 52, 64, 66, 73, 75, 76, 84, 85 (pitcher), 88, 94, 96, 98
Erik Kvalsvik: cover, pages 29, 49
Rolland White: pages 6, 25, 27, 36, 37, 51, 53, 61, 69, 72, 77, 85 (book), 95, 97
Photograph courtesy Library of Congress, Washington, D.C.: page 30 (knife)

Edited by Frances K. Stevenson and Dru Dowdy
Designed and composed by Polly Franchine, Washington, D.C., and electronically typeset in ITC Walbaum
Printed on eighty-pound Warren's Lustro Offset Enamel by Schneidereith and Sons, Baltimore, Maryland